THE COUNTRY DIARY BOOK OF
DECORATING
English Country Style

THE COUNTRY DIARY BOOK OF
DECORATING
English Country Style

Sydney A Sykes

ARCADE PUBLISHING · NEW YORK

LITTLE, BROWN AND COMPANY

To Annette and Oliver

First U.S. Edition

Library of Congress Cataloging-in-Publication Data

Sykes, Sydney A., 1943-
The country diary book of decorating : English country style /
Sydney A. Sykes.
    p. cm.
ISBN 1-55970-079-3
1. Interior decoration—England.   2. Decoration and ornament—
England.   3. Country homes—England.   I. Title.
NK2043.S95   1990
747.22—dc20   89-17934 CIP

The publishers would like to thank Rowena Stott, Edith Holden's
great-niece and copyright holder of this work,
who has made the publication of this book possible.

Published in the United States by Arcade Publishing, Inc., New York,
a Little, Brown company

Originally published in Great Britain by
Webb & Bower (Publishers) Ltd., Exeter, Devon.

10 9 8 7 6 5 4 3 2 1

Designed by Ron Pickless

PRINTED IN HONG KONG

Frontispiece: Painted clock dial from a late nineteenth-century long-case clock

CONTENTS

ROOM-BY-ROOM GUIDE

INTRODUCTION

Country living is the simple comfort of traditional pleasures: the picture of an old-world cottage with timber frames enthusing oak-beamed heritage; of thatch and rustic charm. The fragrance of honeysuckle rose and lavender in the wild floral garden, and the aromatic smells of the herb garden epitomize the essence of Country Style. The current popularity of country furnishings has its roots in the rural traditions of yesteryear. Contemporary English Country Style portrays the best of those appealing traditions. When we live in harmony with nature, we are living according to our common heritage; if we stick with this philosophy the products with which we surround ourselves display little or nothing to offend the eye.

Country Style decoration is not confined to inside the home – it is equally appropriate out of doors. Authentic Country Style is a subtle blend of harmony and contrasts. In the natural world there are the wild flowers and the woodland trees; the grassy meadows and the waving fields of corn; the hills and valleys; the blue-dappled skies and the greens and browns of the landscape – all obvious examples of natural contrast. These variations which are common to the natural environment form the backbone of English Country Style – its familiar expression of colour and design, combined with an informal simplicity are powerful temptations for the would-be home decorator.

The love of growing and tending plants, whether green fern or flowering begonia, in flowerpot, tub, window-box or conservatory, has endured through the ages. The natural softness that foliage gives to a room is an essential ingredient of Country Style. The desire to capture the richness and fragrance of the garden within the house is the corner-stone of many contemporary design schemes, and the English love of the garden, and of gardening, is one of the most fundamental traits of the national character. Beautiful flowers provoke an enthusiasm for life and are indicative of a caring and sensitive attitude.

One of the greatest gifts of a perfect cottage garden is the gift of solitude, a feeling of perfect restfulness and peace. Alas, not everyone has the space for the magical cottage plot, which offers such infinite pleasure to the owner, and to all who pass by. However, to maintain a certain harmony with nature and to create a colourful sense of tranquillity within the home, ensure that house plants abound in profusion and variety.

Country Style ingredients, therefore, comprise a good dose of romance, mixed with nostalgia; a high degree of workmanship and simple elegance; volumes of charm; a modicum of wit, mixed and stirred with memories of a bygone age; plus a healthy respect for the integrity of past craftsmanship, the inheritance of which it embraces. Add to all these ingredients twentieth-century technology, the talents of today's artists and designers who, with flair and creativity, fuse these talents with style and colour to create the heart of English Country Style.

Once created, this decorating style, which is full of appealing traditions which typically promote attention to care and detail, instills a feeling of restful reassurance. When you have become acquainted with the mature virtues and unpretentious beauty of Country Style, this book will illustrate how you can create a little bit of the countryside wherever you may live. It is a decorating style which can transcend and transform any home, be it a London mews or an industrial cottage; a town house or a new estate; a country seat or a two-roomed bedsit. The mood remains comfortably consistent. *The Country Diary Book of Decorating* illustrates numerous finished solutions to a variety of decorating problems, and emphasizes that the joy of English Country Style is its timelessness and adaptability, which in turn allows enormous scope for experimentation when you begin to make your own contribution to interior design.

In today's high-tech world of plastic and chrome – materials that are artificial and values that are superficial – it is not surprising that upon reflection the tendency is towards a return to old-fashioned values and simple, practical solutions which are functional as well as being pleasing to the eye. The love of pine is today strong in all its manifestations: simple wooden spoons; doors, floors and boxes; a well-scrubbed table, wash-stand or dresser – originally painted, later stripped or simply stencilled. Equally popular are cooking utensils in clay, copper and tin; similarly the collecting of craft goods and antiques, both novel and practical, is much in vogue. Hand-worked embroideries, picture samplers, fire-screens and carvings illustrating the touch of the human hand, and all reflecting years of treasured use, have become sought-after accessories.

The demand for original material, plus the increasing interest in hand-made crafts, has led to a revival in the growth of craft centres where interest can be stimulated, curiosity aroused and skills studied. The artisan can demonstrate his craft, and people can buy the product from potter, glass-blower, carpenter or painter – decorative or practical items that enhance the home and reward the talents of the contemporary craftsman.

Anything that says country craft adds a flavour of the past to the home. Fragile items of pottery or glass, too delicate to leave out in the room, can form an ideal decorative focus when displayed in a cabinet. An old ceramic pitcher makes an attractive vase when filled with dried flowers, and a wash bowl becomes functional when displayed with fresh fruit. Even an old piece of industrial equipment, be it a spinning wheel or a loom shuttle, can add a flavour of the past to your home and enhance that lived-in look. Accessories do not have to be old, nor do they have to be hand-made, to provide an old-fashioned country feeling. Practical and decorative reproductions of barometers, clocks, boxes, trays, tin-ware and ceramics can be used to good effect in the home. All these items are widely available, usually less expensive and easier to find than originals, and are appropriate for today's Country Style homes.

Collections are a very personal accessory and blend well with any room display, be they pottery jugs, mugs or Staffordshire figures, glass bottles, plates or wooden spoons. Anything from butterflies, samplers, button hooks, silver-top scent bottles or birds in domes will enhance the interior decor of any room, given a degree of creative restraint.

Over the past decade the best-selling book *The Country Diary of an Edwardian Lady* has influenced many aspects of our chosen way of life. When it was first published in 1977, it reintroduced much which had been felt to be lacking in the modern city-orientated life-styles of its readers, who yearned to return to the simple, natural beauty of Edith Holden's world, as depicted in the wonderfully fresh watercolours which illustrate her diary. The book inspired a television series and became the basis of the world's first ever and biggest co-ordinated collection of home furnishings.

The Country Diary Book of Decorating shows readers how to recreate this countrified charm in their own homes. Over one hundred colour photographs illustrate the potential of English Country Style when applied to even the most modest home. The emphasis, as with all things in the *Country Diary* genre, is on a simple picturesque style, which draws on nature as the chief inspirational force. The colours, tones, shapes and images of the seasons provide the framework for the book and, as shown in summary below, the essence of Country Style.

All these colour moods and highlights of nature's year are the very essence of English Country Style. This style takes its inspiration from nature; but like nature which can be wild and unruly, ever changing and unpredictable, so the decorative results are less refined. There are simple solutions, not to structure or restrict like nature itself, and always with that element of surprise. In fact the real joy is in its innocence – the layering of design patterns, flowers, prints and colours in an unstructured appearance. To be seen as unrelated by scale but related by *colour* is a direct measure of the decorator's artistry – combining imagination and inspiration from the natural environment to create an interior room or decorative solution using nature's living pigments as a palette.

THE FRESHNESS OF SPRING

Just as nature's seasons unfold, so will the contents of this book, opening with the arrival of spring's burst of sun-colours and closing with winter's pale shades. These pages will record the natural transition through the seasons, noting the changing colours and showing how the natural calendar affects our thinking, enhances our environment and provides a rich source of reference for our interior decorations.

Nature's calendar is indelibly stamped on the diary of human activities. With the coming of spring and the first hints of a change in the weather, homes that have been a retreat from the elements become open and accessible. Gardens start to show signs of life, animals and insects emerge from hibernation and the return of swifts and swallows and the bleat of new-born lambs are tangible indicators of better things to come.

May Day is traditionally the last of the series of rites celebrating the arrival of spring. In medieval England it was the custom to bedeck houses with hawthorn blossoms and sweet-smelling herbs. To 'Go a Maying' was a popular pastime characterized by boisterous enthusiasm. The May Queen was the prettiest girl in the village, and the May Pole was hung with floral tributes and ribbons of brightly coloured braids to celebrate the

Roman festival of flowers in dance and music. Sadly few of these charming country celebrations of nature's freely given gifts have survived the industrial age; where they remain their true meaning is invariably forgotten or misplaced. However, while the great feast of Easter is the corner-stone of Christian belief, the spirit of hope and rebirth will prevail.

The milder spring temperatures increase our levels of activity after a winter of enforced retirement. It is a time to spring-clean and bring to fruition those home-decorating ideas hatched during long, dark evenings in front of the fire. Springtime is the great liberator: lighter, longer evenings allow more time in the garden, and inside the consequences of winter confinement are all too apparent. Halls, stairs, landings and living-rooms show obvious signs of wear and tear, and those unwelcome by-products of open fires and central heating – dirt and dust – are cruelly exposed.

In tune with nature we are greatly influenced by the natural rhythms of the season and with the advent of spring we too seek to rebuild, refurbish and start afresh. Manufacturers and retailers respond to the prevailing mood, and winter ranges are cleared to make way for the spring season's fashions, styles and colours. The professional designer rationalizes these seasonal influences and takes account of numerous practical considerations, such as, the cost of fibre or the finished fabric, printing techniques and the technology associated with dyes and finishes. Colour is probably the primary purchasing consideration. A change in colour is often the first obvious indicator of a new season's palette. Each year will have its essential throw-away colours but a good design, with a durable, timeless quality, best reflects nature's consistent traditions. In essence it can be summed up thus: fashion is fickle but good, classic design lasts for ever.

Products that are small, changeable and inexpensive, such as table-clothes, cushions, lampshades – even notepaper, tissues and towels – create an opportunity to experiment with different colours. It is not so easy to rectify errors of judgement over the choice of carpets, suites and wallpaper. Colours are affected by their surroundings, by the light source and by adjacent furnishings. A small paint chip illustrated on a manufacturer's paint card beside hundreds of others, will look entirely different on an expanse of wall. Harsh store lighting is very misleading. The carpet which looks greeny-grey under fluorescent lighting in the shop, may look bluish-green in your sitting-room. It may seem like stating the obvious, but too few people take advantage of fabric and paint samples. Careful scrutiny of samples of soft furnishings and wallpaper fabrics in the comfort of the home is a good way of avoiding problems which arise later. Similarly, always test your choice of paint colour on a small section of the wall before committing to the complete scheme. A well-disciplined approach to interior design increases your knowledge, improves your judgement and consequently makes the whole process a rewarding, rather than a frustrating, exercise.

A spring garden is a living demonstration of harmony of colour and texture and, conversely, great contrast. It can teach us much about the use of colour and its scope and influence in interior design. Traditional spring flowers such as daffodils, primroses, tulips, crocuses and violets are characterized by strong, vibrant colours and a cheerful disposition. The overriding message of a spring garden is optimism. The following pages demonstrate the interpretation of the message of spring in home decoration. Inspirational design ideas for all the rooms in the house and, that vital transitional zone, the garden room mirror the natural environment and illustrate to best advantage the fundamental characteristics of English Country Style.

THE FULL BLOOM OF SUMMER

The full bloom of summer is our reward for a spring spent in caring. The English rose greets the summer garden with a profusion of colour and perfume and our doors and windows are thrown open to allow the season's intoxicating atmosphere to envelop us and our homes.

In the cottage garden, heavily laden fruit trees and bushes bow under their luscious harvest of soft fruits and berries for the making of jams, preserves and cider. The cottage garden becomes a living tapestry as butterflies alight on blooms and blossoms. The air is vibrant with insects and birds whose song sweetens the heady air.

Since earliest times, the cottage garden was the provider of essential produce to fodder man, cow or pig. Hens who scratched around the porch and doorway were the providers of eggs. Slowly, however, the country garden took on a new form. As priorities and needs changed, land was gradually cultivated for orchard fruits and herbs, and grass around the cottage door became cut into beds. Although vegetables still occupied a substantial amount of the garden space, more attention was given to fruits and later to a considerable variety of flowers. Indeed in the country-house garden, fruits were not only cultivated for their edible values but for the beauty of their blossoms.

From cottage gardens being areas of food production, increasing numbers became cultivated as areas of restfulness and seclusion: an aesthetic oasis. Paths were gravelled, grassed or flagged, adding structure and division to areas for cultivation; walls were built to sit on, look over, confine and separate. Flowers were grown for their beauty and scent, colour and variety – the English cottage garden had come into its own. No matter how grand or small the plot may be, a garden is a delightful and cherished possession.

A conservatory is an asset to any home, offering added spaciousness for a variety of uses and forming a link between nature's elements and the organized privacy of our homes – garden rooms are areas of transition.

With the coming of summer our thoughts turn to revamping the exterior of the house. A spell of fine, settled weather provides the opportunity for windows and doors to be left ajar to allow paint to dry. A newly painted home is shown to best advantage in the strong summer sunlight and creates the perfect background for al fresco eating. Inside, decorating schemes will inevitably reflect the colours of the season; there is greater impetus to throw off natural reserve and choose bold, vibrant statements – both of colour and design.

Summer is traditionally a time for taking the annual holiday to guaranteed sun. The result of many an excursion to distant lands is the stimulus it gives to our creative mind. When we gain knowledge of other countries, taste their food and wines, experience their culture and heritage, explore their art and antiquity and savour their craft and colour we are subconsciously filing away ideas and broadening our capacity for imaginative thought. We return stimulated by these new ideas and are excited by the possibility of breaking out of a hitherto rather formal approach to home decoration.

There is much to encourage the traveller to break from the conservative tradition when thoughts turn to home decoration but it is wise to be prudent over the practical application of ideas gleaned from different cultures and different climates. Recreating a Provençal sitting-room in deepest England without regard to the inherent influences is a dangerous game. Introduce holiday-inspired schemes gradually and limit the effect – be sparing and subtle and the result will be pleasing to the eye.

There is, however, no need to explore the countries of the world for inspiration, the summer garden is one source of rich examples of the ways in which colours affect our perceptions. Interior decoration can become less of a chore if we take a lesson from our natural surroundings for the summer in full bloom provides us with a unique opportunity for study.

THE RICHNESS OF AUTUMN

The autumn pleasures of the countryside will take you into a world of rich colour – a warm autumnal tapestry of hue and shade. Hazel-nuts, 'conkers', blackberries, rose hips, elderberries and the early mountain-ash berries glow in clusters bright as fluorescent beads. Orange, which belongs to the earth tones, is the one colour that epitomizes the 'Fall'. Blazing foliage, where rusts, reds and oranges predominate, reflect a baked, worn comfort. These natural colours of pottery convey the richness of the earth.

The colour term 'orange' is derived from the fruit. It is clearly evident that nature serves as an inspiration for the various colours and textures we have at our disposal through the wide ranges of wall-coverings, fabrics, floor-coverings and hand-made crafts. A tangible richness can be created using the mature colours of autumn as your palette.

Because of the 'hearth and home' association of warmth and comfort it is not surprising that orange and brown earth tones are popular choices for kitchen decor. A country kitchen, in either pine or oak, is the ideal place to let your imagination run riot. Fill the open shelves with objects that are both functional and attractive and yet stimulate intrigue and enquiry. Collect to a theme or a specific period but always aim to

create the warm, nostalgic ambience of a Country Style kitchen.

Autumn is a season of superstition – the twilight zone of the year. On Michaelmas Day the devil was cast out from Heaven and it is said that any fruit gathered after this date will be made tasteless. Saint Michael is revered as the protector against the devil and the guide to Heaven. Autumn is the time of the apple harvest; there are many traditions, superstitions and ancient folk lore associated with the apple – the first fruit of temptation.

Autumn is a time of fires. Halloween fires are built and the farmer will torch the fields to cleanse the ground for new crops and to drive off goblins and warlocks. The Halloween pumpkin guards against witches on the day of the dead – All Souls. Saint Catherine was burnt at the wheel in November and on 5th November bonfires are lit and effigies are burnt to commemorate Guy Fawkes' infamous plot of 1605.

Autumn is a time for gathering in – the grain harvest, fruit picking and winter logs and kindlewood. It is traditionally a season for stock-taking of cattle, sheep and stores. This natural response to the turning of the seasons is reflected in our homes and gardens. Attention once more is focused on interior decoration as shortening days and cooler temperatures put an end to outside chores. If the essence of Country Style is the inspiration and influence of the natural environment, then autumn is the season which most closely equates with the true spirit of County Style – harmony with nature. The colours, tones and textures of autumn are the trademarks of the season and introduce a rich, warm sense of security when recreated in decoration themes for the home.

THE CRISPNESS OF WINTER

In winter the landscape is at rest, and in our homes thoughts are of contemplation and celebration, for winter to every child means the coming of Christmas, the birth of Christ and religious joy and the giving and receiving of gifts. In winter it was the custom for villagers to gather all that was still green – shining holly and variegated ivy leaves. Holly was for foresight, ivy for fidelity. Both would keep evil spirits at bay until Candlemas Eve. Mistletoe was magical, in ancient law a ward against evil, a cure for epilepsy and an aid to fertility. Holly and mistletoe are symbols of immortality, a source of comfort in winter, berry bright in the darkest days of the year.

The holly still makes a traditional display in many a hallway or as a table decoration at Christmas and the New Year. But today, where bright colours are *de rigueur*, and colour television feasts our eyes, it has lost most, though not all, of the magical effect it had in years gone by.

Christmas and Thanksgiving mean reflection, consideration, kindness and caring for family and friends and those not so fortunate at this time of year. In northern Europe yule-logs were burnt in honour of Odin and Thor. The word 'yule' comes from Jul, the ancient name of the Thor festival, in contemporary Swedish it is the word for Christmas.

The festival of Christmas is regarded as the greatest celebration in the Christian ecclesiastical year. It is a joyous and yet solemn time; the geniality and friendship of the Christmas season in England has long been a national characteristic.

This is the time of the winter solstice (21st December). As winter approaches, the days become shorter and the weather damper and colder – there is a clean emptiness to the landscape. When I think of winter I chiefly think of silence. On a still day, especially if it is frosty, a snow-scened country walk is often disturbingly silent. The sound of a twig snapping underfoot will set a wood pigeon clattering away among the bare oaks. We often say, somewhat perversely, how we enjoy winter; but what we really mean is that we enjoy feeling sheltered against it. Indoors is where most of us like to be, warming ourselves against an open fire.

In winter we pull down the shutters on our homes. Decorative activity is at a very low ebb, but imaginations will continue to work overtime. Thinking of all those jobs you meant to do, and all those you are planning to do next year will keep the adrenalin flowing. For winter is the best time to plan new decorative ideas, extensions to the home, alterations and new design schemes.

More than any other decorative ingredient you choose for this room, colour will dictate its personality. Choice of colour scheme is the most important and least expensive item on your shopping list. It is also the most difficult factor for many would-be home decorators to cope with, because your choice of colour must come first. During the winter months consider carefully all the options so that you are on top of the situation when the decorative cycle begins again in the spring.

Once you have decided upon the colour scheme, then choose the fabrics, wallpaper, paint and accessories to match. To settle on the correct theme, or colour scheme, you have to understand the effect of colour and how it works in a room.

Remember that colour has a personality – basically every colour is either warm or cool. Yellow, peach, red and spring green will impose their bright personality on a room. Conversely, the cool tones of green, burgundy, taupe and blue will lower the visual temperature and activity level in a room.

The seasonal changes of nature's palette can provide clear illustrations of how a room can be decorated to suit changing moods and circumstances. The colours of winter are bright and sharp in contrast: bright green of holly; red of berries, hip and robin's breast; white of snow and frost; brown and grey of hedgerow and field.

Nature herself is infinitely patient, resilient and varied, and with your decorating ideas variety and harmony can be achieved with care, imagination and patience. Do not be in a hurry to reach a solution, attend to every detail and you will not be disappointed with the decorative result.

Pretence can be great fun, like charades, pretend you are going to redecorate a room in your home; think it through as you make pictures in the flames of the fire.

It is a good idea to close your eyes and imagine the room totally bare, right down to the walls, ceiling and floor. Now start to build a colour scheme, beginning with what you see as the end result. What changes would you make? How do you want the room to feel? More, or less formal? Traditional or contemporary? Warm and cosy or cool and spacious? Lively and invigorating or calm and relaxing? What about lighting? Consider power points and plugs, lighting positions and usage. Remember that lighting effects around the home must be appropriate for working, relaxing and entertaining.

SPRING

SPRING

I heard a thousand blended notes
While in a grove I sat reclined;
In that sweet mood when pleasant thoughts,
Bring sad thoughts to the mind;

To her fair works did Nature link
The human soul that through me ran
And much it grieved my heart to think
What man has made of man.

Through primrose tufts in that green bower
The periwinkle trailed it's wreathes,
And 'tis my faith that every flower
Enjoys the air it breathes.

The birds around me hopped and played,
Their thoughts I cannot measure, —
But the least motion which they made,
It seemed a thrill of pleasure.

The budding twigs spread out their fan
To catch the breezy air
And I must think, do all I can,
That there was pleasure there.

If this belief from heaven be sent,
If such be Nature's holy plan
Have I not reason to lament
What man has made of man?

'Lines written in early spring'. W. Wordsworth

The freshness of spring is most easily illustrated in the seasonal flowers: periwinkles, violets and fresh green leaves; yellow daffodils, primrose blossoms, anemones and bluebells, soft scents and mellow colours. Bird song heralds the passing of winter; it is possible to identify thrush, blackbird, hedge sparrow, skylark, blue tit, chaffinch and wagtail. The snow attempts to linger and in so doing adds a clean white background to emphasize the freshness of the colours. Spring cleaning provides the decorator with the opportunity to refresh, adapt or change the furnishings, designs and colours of a room, adding springtime freshness to bedrooms, bathrooms, hallways and stairs.

Above

Simplicity is the use of natural materials – Country Style's corner-stone. From earliest times, solid floors were widely made of baked, dampened or beaten earth. During the seventeenth and eighteenth centuries kiln bricks were used, and later these were replaced by stone flags. However, some of these were laid directly on to the earth and may therefore give rise to dampness. Part of the floor's charm is its unevenness.

Left

Hallways are often transient areas of the house: you simply move through the space, to get from one place to another.
However, a method of achieving a degree of elegance is to position a wing chair to allow you to pause and rest or await company for that spring walk, or a majestic long-case clock will set the tone and time in an otherwise rather austere setting. A practical tile pattern on the floor provides freshness all the year round.

Opposite

These are reflections of bygone days: spring sunshine sparkling on a picket-tiled Victorian hallway, rich in beautiful oak panelling which was used to line the walls. Some can be richly carved, but here simple boarded panels have been used conveying warmth of character, a welcoming environment important in any hallway.
The reef curtain is tied back during daylight hours, but drawn in the evening for privacy, and to stop draughts along the corridor. One lovely piece of furniture can set the proper tone – here a traditional, old dough bin has been used as a side table, for odds and ends, keys, gloves or a place to write notes and leave messages. The panelling and decorative elements on the staircase are typical of the grand houses of the eighteenth century.

Opposite

Consider your kitchen's assets as well as its liabilities. Does it have any redeeming features? For example, as here, wall surface and texture detail of brickwork, architectural beams, cupboards – all can be repainted or stripped back to their natural stage. Tiles or flooring might be worth saving for incorporating into your new decor. A feature window can give good light for practical illumination on work surfaces. A small area can be made to appear quite large when, as here, fresh clean white and yellow are used dramatically to create an illusion of space. This is maintained by minimal clutter. Practical objects only occupy premium space. Simple shapes, practical cooking appliances, painted white wood, garden furniture and storeroom shelving, white-tiled flooring which ensures a timeless quality of simple charm – all are very effective. If space is a problem, then think what could be done elsewhere, or what could be moved out. Perhaps your wash-room could be located in the room next door. Perhaps the freezer could go in the garage, the refrigerator to a back hallway or porch, or, as here, a previously unused back scullery can be given a fresh new look for cooking and casual dining.

Above

The art of decorating your kitchen today is to recapture successfully the 'best of the old' in a style of today, to create a working environment that is completely harmonious. In this kitchen pine-fitted units provide a practical solution to storage. Extra cupboards and shelves have been fitted to avoid unsightly, inaccessible corners, shelves have been added between wall-units and work surfaces to increase storage and are used for the general clutter of jars, fruit and herbs, spice jars assorted china jugs, mugs, plates, kitchen scales and brass weights – dried flowers provide decorative interest. Pine has also been introduced as a bridge to create continuity in the form of a splash back decorative feature. The practical green and cream 'picket' checkboard tile flooring has been highlighted in the detail of the cooker surround and hood. Co-ordinating wallpaper and paint complete the harmony and provide a practical and decorative solution to the kitchen decoration problem. Informal dining is made possible with a circular pine table and chairs. The cream and green colour theme is retained with a decorative table-cloth, tableware and details such as cutlery and a candle in a turned pine candlestick.

Above

Large country houses of the eighteenth century had larder, pantry and kitchen or servant areas flagged with stone or quarry tiles. Early country-house kitchens typically had high-beamed ceilings to extract the smoke and cooking smells when emanated from below. These floors varied in colour depending on the locality and availability of local stone; warm-coloured tiles make a solid floor less unitarian, and they look more inviting still, as here, with a richly coloured woven rug. Sparseness and simplicity can complement the architectural features of the house. The large dark oak beams are allowed to dominate the decorative effect of the white-washed kitchen. Furniture has been left in its natural colour of stripped pine and mahogany – simple uncluttered practical charm. Walls can be a giant canvas on which to hang clutter and embellishments of tapestries and paintings. The impulse to over decorate can, however, be resisted to give a feeling of spaciousness and practicality.

Opposite

In Victorian times the conservatory was purely for the nurturing and rearing of plants and flowers. Today it has a more versatile use. As the daylight hours begin to lengthen in springtime, so breakfasts or dinners can quite happily be eaten in these cosy surroundings. Conservatories have an abundance of light so giving a feeling of space and freshness. Plants in pots or trained on a trellis diffuse the sunlight so giving a softness to the dining area. Country pine, wicker chairs and baskets, together with a simple circular table are all you need to create this extra dining area. The latter can be covered with table-linen in a pretty meadow-flower print, thus creating a floral focus on which to place fruit, cheese, wine or fresh cut flowers. The addition of a large mirror on the wall gives an illusion of extra light and space to what is in reality a small confined area. This space serves as a sunny breakfast room, or additional dining-room, a den, study or children's playroom.

Above
Today's country kitchen is not too far removed from what it was like in bygone days: a place of country cooking, good wholesome food, warmth and nourishment – a great storehouse. The country kitchen has always been the larder: fresh baked pies, fresh fruit made into jams and jellies, strawberry and cream, seasoning and spices. In most modern homes, food preparation, eating space, laundry utilities and storage are partitioned into separate areas, but in older country cottages, where the kitchen was truly the hub of the house, these were incorporated into one large undivided room. The kitchen dresser was a remarkable piece of furniture, containing not only food and household supplies, but jugs, plates, mugs, storage jars, baskets, rolling pins, tins, spices and many other foodstuffs and practical collections of kitchen gadgets and utensils. Glass bottles and fruit jars stood on window sills, and tin and copper saucepans hung from the ceiling beams. The kitchen constantly resounded to a clatter of chopping, beating, whipping and stirring. Bountiful was the food and potent was the flavour and fragrance, not only from wholesome cooking, but from flowers, fresh cut or dried. Herbs collected and used decoratively add colour and the sweet smells of the passing seasons to your home.

Opposite below

Not all country items have to be made of old timber planks, with original woodworm and authentic stains of heritage. The country look can be achieved with carefully selected modern furniture that retains closely the traditional values, and practical proportions of the originals. In fact, many modern dressers can be made to look stunning with careful consideration of colour and style. Many original country pieces were painted, lined or stencilled, most dressers had panelled backs and small bung handles. So elegance can be achieved without age. But clutter is an essential ingredient to convey that country feeling. The artistic touch can be lovingly arranged with the correct mixture of authentic and modern pieces, pottery or china of today with mementos of the past. Country is adaptable and practical. Today a wide variety of old and modern reproduction dressers are available. As well as being one of the most authentic and attractive ways of furnishing your cottage-style kitchen, the dresser is a most efficient provider of cupboards, drawers and display shelves, while retaining individuality and style.

Above

In complete contrast to white walls and spacious practicality, here charm and cosiness has been achieved with warm pinks and delicate pastel prettiness that makes this kitchen a personal delight in which to work or eat. All the same ingredients are available – practical shelves, functional clutter, spices, storage, specially designed units to fit the available space, but gone is the scrubbed kitchen table, rustic sink and clinical whiteness. Here is a personal kitchen of delights, retaining all the charm of the country, as this is obviously a cook's kitchen as every corner is utilized with functional items. This small kitchen remains true to its humble heritage, but with special displays of country wicker baskets and dried flowers hanging from the ceiling, and floral prints to add colour and style, plus stencilled cornice details on the walls and feminine frills on curtain treatments. This kitchen is a private place of creation, where wholesome food awaits the cook's attentive hands.

Above

It is strangely ironic that the English, who pride themselves on their cleanliness and for being a civilized society, were so slow to establish a clean household. Even after the Roman occupation of Britain, which lasted over three hundred years (during which time the Romans repeated their sanitary accomplishment at home by building a network of plumbing systems, baths and aqueducts, both public and private) these civilized customs did not take hold in Britain and for almost a thousand years there was hardly a tap to turn in Britain. By the end of the eighteenth century improvements in heating and lighting were accompanied by improvements in sanitation. The shower bath was invented, bath tubs replaced the elegant cold-water plunge pools, and most important of all, a really efficient water closet, fitted with valves that worked, became available at last.

In this bathroom the blue, white and cream colour scheme creates a tangible freshness; the same colours in fixed painted modern bathroom fixtures have been used in an old timber-framed home to combine modern amenities with country charm and rustic splendour. Window drapes hide storage clutter in dresser cupboards; blue and white ceramics can be featured as a decorative collection, forming a pleasing display and creating a period atmosphere.

Opposite

The finished surface reflects the true country decor. Here a painted wooden floor provides a practical solution to a bathroom floor, either polished or given a clear varnish finish. Water can be simply wiped up and removed. Rush and wicker make ideal furniture and matting as steam and moisture have little effect on their structural soundness. Fabrics and embroidered co-ordinating towels, robes and printed shower curtains can add the finishing touches to your decorative scheme. They soften a room, whether in a smart masculine ticking stripe for a practical tailored look, or, as featured here, in a small chintz floral on matching wallpaper, shower curtain and window drapes to give a fresh, romantic tone. Co-ordinating ceramics and a free-standing colourful tub, give a traditional Victorian flavour to a large area. Plants or cut flowers interspersed with collective clutter, give a springtime fragrance, and there is a natural freshness in the co-ordinating yellows, creams, whites and greens. Decorative accessories add an intricate sense of detailing to this eclectically styled bathroom. Victorian accessories blend well with country decor. Soap dishes, jug and bowl, tooth-brush holders, shampoo and scent bottles make ideal collectables, adding atmosphere as well as practical storage for soaps, bath salts or pot-pourri.

Opposite
Today, a country-style bathroom is once again more of a room. It may not yet be as large and spacious as its Victorian counterpart but it will at least be more comfortable, and better decorated. Shelves and bath surrounds will contain plants, toiletries, china, soaps and decorative objects. Walls will be mainly tiles, panelled to match the bath, or wallpapered (with washable or glazed paper for practicality) or painted decoratively, with tiles or wallpaper frieze to add detail and convey style. Many will, ironically, be as cluttered as the Victorian bathrooms, and reflect traditional fixtures and fittings in brass, ceramic and tile that convey an eclectic love of memorabilia. Plants can be decoratively featured as most bathrooms today have good light windows, and the mixture of warmth, moisture, water and steam, make an ideal atmosphere for plant growth. The greatest luxury will be special to this century, that of a fitted carpet, rug or co-ordinating bath set to suit the decor and colours, and provide a feeling of softness and warmth. A far cry from the cold, damp, unwelcoming space of early bathrooms, yet in typical country style reflecting the traditions of the past.

Above
A collection of prints or paintings can look stunning when displayed in a high-ceilinged bathroom. Angled rooms can also be highlighted by using striped wallpaper to illustrate dramatically the changes in direction and the sculptural angle unique to a space. If this decorative feature is employed then simplicity must also follow, particularly in the amount of accessories used in the finishing touches. Too much clutter will destroy the spaciousness created. Floral chintz curtains will be all that you need to complete the look, allowing winter sunshine to bring the freshness and natural light to sparkle on white tiles and brass bath fittings.

Left
The elegance of the English manor house can be successfully created with the addition of library shelving or period bookcases. Many large houses of the eighteenth century had a grand library room for quiet study and reflection, a room filled with history and tradition. Today, families need a private retreat away from the formality of living-and dining-rooms. This can be a family den, or study, a casual space in which to read, play games or simply to enjoy good conversation. As these studies will be a storehouse for clutter, books and pastimes, hobbies and collections, the best results will come from keeping the walls simple by using wallpaper or paint; attractive chairs or table-cloth can add colour, but books can be colourful accessories too.

Opposite
The elaborate trellis co-ordinated wallcovering acts as a busy foil to the sturdy traditional chintz fabric. This becomes the focal point in this elegant study and is exemplary of the Victorian theme. Unlike its Victorian counterpart this room is light, bright and airy. The complementary rose print continues the room detail. Your choice of accessories will be guided by the degree of formality you wish to convey. Here the Victorian inspiration is continued with an old brass oil lamp, with delicate glass globe, Staffordshire figures and ceramic jugs and pitcher, the latter, decorated with a harmonizing rose decoration and filled with natural flowers.

Below
Mingling the old with the new can be both experimental and distinctive. For instance, as here, an old-fashioned inglenook hearth, in a traditional country cottage with low ceiling beams and simply painted washed walls, has been enhanced by a striking checker-board tiled flooring that creates contrasts in a sensitive manner. Simple solutions can add distinctive drama.

The main purpose in a sitting-room is to create a relaxed and enjoyable sitting area, so the decor and colours should successfully blend to create country-style comfort. In this drawing-room springtime yellow has been used to dramatic effect in a contemporary cabbage rose print, with a co-ordinating stipple texture. Co-ordinating wallcovering and frieze offer a mix-and-match opportunity. The textured wallpaper provides a background for decorative prints, while the wallpaper border, used both high and low, provides a framework to the room. Simple (pinched centre) fabric creates an attractive 'boxed' pelmet; both fabrics can be used for pinch pleats and fabric accessories. The wicker table has been painted green to emphasize the leaf colour featured in the fabric, and the table setting is completed with matching yellow and pink roses. Superb flower arrangements whether natural, silk or artificial can reflect the season's colours and highlight fabric colours, thus creating harmony and style.

Today's market offers a wealth of designer co-ordinated fabrics. This pre-planned array of colours and textures that all work together presents the interior designer/decorator with an overwhelming abundance of choice. However, a balance of creativity, co-ordination and orginality can be achieved with a few careful considerations. There is much more to choosing a window dressing than simply selecting a cover-up. Budget is a prime consideration. Perhaps the window is a unique shape – this will also influence your design direction. Much also depends on the view, for you may wish to frame a picture with fabric swags and fancies, or discreetly add privacy and seclusion to a room. But whether your view is totally private or spectacular, a bare window without fabric is nearly always undistinguished and undesirable. The treatment chosen for the window shown above may be a little over the top, but it makes the point that windows need not be ignored – they can be a vital part of an interior design scheme.

CREATIVE CURTAINS

The Grand Room
Left
Here the curtain treatment provides the focal point in a grand living-room. The window seat gains importance with a triple swag treatment. Each window is framed in a length of fabric that has been pulled through a pair of rings and gently swagged. This treatment requires minimal fabric, hardware or even sewing, yet offers a high-styled look. Swags can add comfort and softness to any room and subdue the harshness of hard edges and lines.

Plain and Fancy
Opposite above
This window treatment combines plain fabric and prints and thereby doubles the effect. A large floral-printed chintz falls in soft folded swags and jabots (which give linings new meaning) while inner draperies of the same fabric are tied back with tasselled cords. These can remain a static decorative feature, for underneath it all is a pair of curtains in a solid plain fabric (in co-ordinating shade and edge trimmed for detail) and these can be drawn for privacy when desired.

Balloon or Festoon Curtain
Below
Today, the balloon or festoon curtain is almost classic. It is a good ingredient for a feminine room, and relatively economical on fabric.

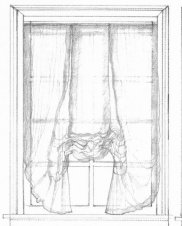
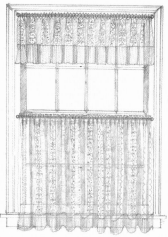

A Lighter Shade of Pale
Above
Here light muslin, lace or organza – all translucent materials – allow maximum light to filter softly into a room, providing the best of both worlds: good light yet affording some degree of privacy. This provides a simple solution which doesn't detract from interesting woodwork and gives a feeling of fresh airy space.

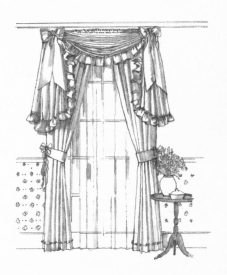

Classical
Above right
This shows how an antique curtain can make a perfect frame for a window or doorway. A ruffle heading on long drape curtains adds a feeling of height and elegance to a room. Fabric tassel edge and tie-back are strong accent features.

Fabric Fancies
Right centre
Pleating, ruffles and frills are all worthy constituents of country style. A pinch-pleated header gathered on to a wooden or brass pole gives that full gathered look. Frill-edged swags can be tied back in romantic bows with long trails for feminine charm. Petite bows attached to hem lines create a pretty hand-finished look.

Medieval or Plantagenet
Right
The Medieval or Plantagenet is a wonderful curtain for that special window – Gothic in essence and traditional in flavour. Tournament pelmet heading, plus pencil pleated curtains – with the addition of woven or embroidered edges – gives the window a monastic look, ancient and antique in richness.

31

CREATIVE CURTAINS

Ruffle Drape or Reef
Left

This ruffle drape is an expensive solution, but well worth the effort if the room needs a highlight. Here, a pleated and frilled valance heads the window – ample fabric swells the curtains, pulled back with frilled tie-backs. The addition of an extra frill at the curtain base deepens the impression of luxury and elegance. The illustrated treatment is in fabric of a single colour but an alternative is Irish lace to give a homespun, traditional appeal of country rooms.

Tie back details
Right

Anything that is long enough can be used as a tie-back, from garlands of flowers, to chains of beads, scarves, cords and tailored fabric. Sometimes, however, the period you are trying to create will dictate the style of the drapes, and the method of tie-back used. To create a classical window it is important to have the correct accessories. Brass knobs to anchor a tie-back reflect the early eighteenth century, whereas an antique corded tie-back with tassel creates a luxurious Victorian 'look'. A romantic bow creates softness and folds for chintz or bedroom window treatments, giving a full, gathered appearance.

Here are six illustrations of the many ways you can achieve the correct look. Many can be adapted and modified and many more can be created given a little imagination.

1 Bow trimmed tie-back
Using a piece of your curtain fabric, or co-ordinating plain satin, measure round the curtain to obtain the back length. Decide on the tie-back width. Make up a plain tie-back separate from the bow, add curtain rings to each end as before, this will allow for the correct tailored look, and maintain a consistent bow at all times. Once created the bow should be pinned in place and tacked on to the shaped tie-back.

2 Filled tie-back with brass rosette knob
The brass knob which can be used on its own is a marvellous way of draping back heavy fabrics, as you simply fold back your curtains over it. This takes the weight off the curtain hooks and provides sound support. However, many additions can be used to create simple variations. Here a filled tie-back has been used in either contrasting or co-ordinating fabric, with a heavy wadding insert to give a padded effect.

3 Striped tie-back
These can be ideal for a more masculine appearance, as plain smartness is what can be achieved. Decide how wide you want your tie-back, and take three or four coloured fabrics and join the stripe together. From heavyweight iron-on interfacing, cut out one piece to the complete tie-back size. Iron on to the reverse side and complete the sewing. This will create a stiff geometric stripe to highlight colours in the room or

create a 'feature' accent. Again a curtain ring will need to be sewn to each end to attach to the wall hook.

4 Antique corded tie-back with tassel

There are many antique shops which have a selection of corded and tasselled tie-backs, and many specialist curtain accessory shops will have modern reproductions. Finding the correct colours in these maybe a problem if the old antique tassels are your preference; sometimes it is better to have the tie-backs first and create the fabrics to match. These create a Victorian appearance and are ideal for woven or tapestry period drapes, heavy chintz or plain velvets.

5 Bound shaped tie-back (with frill)

Obtain length required as before. On a sheet of paper mark a strip about 12cm (4¾in) wide by half the length measurement. (Gently shape the curve both sides of the strip so one end is narrowed down to about 4cm (1½in) and cut out the pattern.) Fold the fabric in half, place the wide end of the pattern against the fabric fold and cut out. Add a heavyweight iron-on interfacing to the fabric reverse as

before. This can then be either kept plain, piped, frilled or enhanced in any way you wish.

6 Plaited tie back

This is a variation on the filled tie-back as three separate filled pieces are used. These can be three different plain colours, or all the same fabric. Sometimes if you have used three co-ordinating fabrics in your room, a mixture of each print can look equally attractive, and create a detail accent at your window.

Smart Wear
Left
This more masculine approach combines a swag with jabots reaching down as far as the window sill, swathed casually over a decorated brass rod and teamed up with a smart but simply stated roman shade in shirting stripe. This not only provides privacy when desired, but also an interesting effect, which can be picked up on accent objects in the room, such as light shades or cushions, and also gives scope for related interplay with wallpapers and border, paint or print.

HEADING TRACKS AND POLES

Looped heading

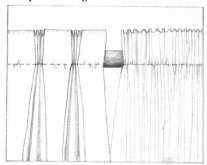

Triple or pinch-pleat tape/Pencil-pleat tape

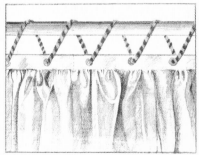

Eyelet heading

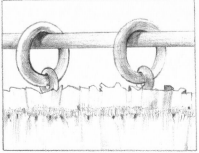

Ringed and shirred heading

CHURCH AND CHAPEL

Left

If the home is the heart of English Country Style, then the parish church or chapel is its soul. The church spire is the centre of the community and few structures can command more reverence and respect. The colour and textures of our lives therefore, cannot be separated from the influences of the church interior which reflects much of our heritage and culture: a display of flowers on lectern stand or altar in spring and summer, or the richness of the harvest golds of autumn, the bright red berries on holly bow displayed over porch in winter. Dark Victorian or medieval glass, reflecting translucent colours on a stone-flagged floor, paintings on plaster walls, screen, organ case or panel, all convey the warmth and cosiness that we all emulate in our home and interiors.

The English church tower or spire is the one symbol which is most missed by the English when travelling in other countries, not because everywhere else is heathen, but because of the unique frequency with which they appear within the English countryside. One cannot travel many miles in England without seeing one, above tree or wood, around a bend in the road, or on a distant horizon. Their place in our landscape conveys sanctuary, stability, heritage and traditional pride. They are the focus for the painter's eye and the centre of our community. Few structures can command more reverence and respect.

Below left

The down-to-earth country practicality of English oak, its heartiness that reflects the sentiment of its craftmanship, does much to convey traditional skills and common sense. The medieval English craftsmen were well equipped with all these skills, and enjoyed such good things as life then offered. Smith, carpenter and mason handled their materials with much love and respect, they coaxed materials and never bullied them. These men were slowly establishing a tradition in design, broadening and deepening skills that had been handed on generation after generation. English achievements were famous, but it was in woodwork that they excelled. The crude chests of the thirteenth and fourteenth centuries were decorated with roundels and figures of chip carving, with an unmistakable affinity of purpose, that sense of apt selection and gay orderliness in the forms of embellishment, which are inseparable ingredients of the English tradition of design. Wood acted sturdily in structural work in beams, or clothing halls, with carved panelling or providing stout and serviceable (but never clumsy) tables and benches. Ornamental devices flowed along beams, panelling, chests and cupboards, variegating the oak surfaces with geometric and naturalistic motifs. Often Gothic architecture was used as an inspiration for intricate tracery, giving to wooden chest or silver caskets a 'hallowed' appeal.

Opposite

With all the activity, chatter and commotion in our halls and entrances they are not parts of the home in which we spend much time, but their effect on other areas is not to be underestimated. The first and most important consideration when decorating the hall is its size – small areas will need to appear larger, so avoid clutter and go for fresh, light paintwork. Are there any architectural features worth detailing within your choice of decor? Such as a beamed ceiling, oak panelling, stain-glass window, dado rail or cornice. The floor or flooring is also a guiding factor in emphasizing a hallway's charm. Perhaps those original flagstones are hidden beneath a plain-coloured fitted carpet, or half disguised by an oriental rug? Remember that halls and entrances are the first points of contact in a home and sympathetic and imaginative decoration will pay dividends.

COUNTRY COLLECTABLES

Above
More permanent displays are best maintained in a glass-fronted cabinet. Groups of objects which are apparently unrelated, but which share a common thread such as colour, shape or texture, can be successfully displayed together. Here various glass bottles, of all shapes and sizes, manage to look cohesive and interesting. There are no clearly defined rules for displaying collectable items, which means plenty of scope for imaginative experimentation.

Above left
The judicious arrangement of treasured collectables, in this case Staffordshire dogs, can turn a blank wall, table top or corner cupboard into an art gallery. Such compositions placed as if arranged on a blank canvas, are as personal as a portrait, and create an important focal point in a room.

Above
Decoy carvings and wild birds have always held a fascination for the avid collector. The decoy carvers experimented endlessly with types of wood and methods of carving and colouring. The art was to create an impression of the bird, rather than an exact replica. Variety in display can be achieved by collecting different types of birds in different materials, from wood, ceramic or clay, and then creating a casual natural display for the shelf or table top.

Opposite above
Victorians were said to abhor a void; they insisted on every inch of their home space being filled with objects, prints, fabrics and textures. Yet, still today, collective clutter means comfortable, emotional richness, as decorative styles often begin as seeds planted in earlier years. Here a fascinating collection of golfing memorabilia gives credence to the belief that most collections emanate from family sentiment – the handing down of old or treasured objects, personal possessions and heirlooms.

Left
This still-life photograph reveals the delicate beauty of Victorian lace, printed chintz and a personal collection of silver and gold.

Right
A cosy armchair corner evokes a feeling of companionship for this display of Victorian dolls. The sentiment is heightened by a beautiful antique Victorian lace bed-cover which has been used as a throw-over coverlet for an old settee. This evokes a whimsical nostalgic mood, that conveys the charm and style of the past.

A very splendid bedroom – the focal point being a particularly handsome bed: a four-poster, draped and bedecked with antique embroidered hangings, offset with plain hangings used behind a shaped headboard and festooned in the elegant casement windows. White lace bedcovers embroidered and fanciful, make the whole room convey a classical timelessness, embroidery again features on the table linen and cushions.

Classical sculptures convey quality and gilt-framed oil paintings complete the picture of grandeur in the best English tradition.

Long table-covers draped to the floor create a feeling of solidity yet glass-topped for practicality. The close unity of pale greens, detailed in the carpet and rug, create a framework for white accents on table-tops and bed-coverings. Soft lemon yellows glow from accent lampshades creating a golden glow to a new spring day.

Left

This photograph shows how the unusual, angled shape of an attic room can be turned into a special feature by allowing the sculptural form of the room to dominate its styling. By using simple whites and creams on the board-plank ceiling and plain plaster walls, the natural daylight can be used to highlight the spaciousness and sculptural qualities of the room. A Victorian cast-iron fireplace has been painted white, an art deco mirror and period reproduction lamps, both pendant and brass, highlight and reflect the sculptural qualities of the room. Peach has been used to relieve the clinical whiteness and to add a warm, soft, mellow tone to the room, on the bedspread, cushions, seating, fabric and in the woven carpet and sampler. Dried flowers and grasses in a peach ceramic jug complete the harmony and illustrate the powerful decorative effect of controlled simplicity.

Above
This fanciful pine-carved Victorian bed
is a craftsman's dream. The
overmantel–headboard has been
enhanced with country floral stencils
which have been repeated on the chair
backs and used decoratively and
exquisitely on the painted chest of
drawers. The decorated bed forms the
focal point in this lovely country-style
bedroom. It is fitted with pretty ruffled
duvet and matching valance, co-
ordinating frilled pillows and is flanked
by a matching pair of table lamps; the
deep full-length curtains and wallpaper
pick up details of the pattern to
reinforce the casual rustic mood of the
room. The plain colours create a feeling
of spaciousness. As one spends up to a
third of one's life in the bedroom it is
wise to think carefully about the decor
and furnishings. Little effort has been
spared here to create a master bedroom
which would take centre stage in the
overall house design.

Right

In this bedroom a rich opulence has been achieved with the use of deep lush co-ordinating fabrics of stripes and flowers, creating a practical tidiness. The room is visually anchored by colour, deep green on a delicately scaled painted iron bed. It is tailored with Oxford square pillowcases, high back drapes in a small-scale matching fabric and a larger swirling tracery print at the mullion window. The fabric has also been used decoratively as chair cushion cover. Simple but effective features include stone and leaded-glass windows and oak beams; country crafted materials are softened by the strong use of colour on the painted furniture and fabrics. An old pine soap box has been converted into a functional bookcase which creates a novel yet practical solution to storage problems. The room's practical nature is reflected by the stripped pine floor, with a wax or clear varnish finish, ideal for youngsters who like to paint or crayon in their rooms. Simple woven rugs retain the crafted mood of practicality.

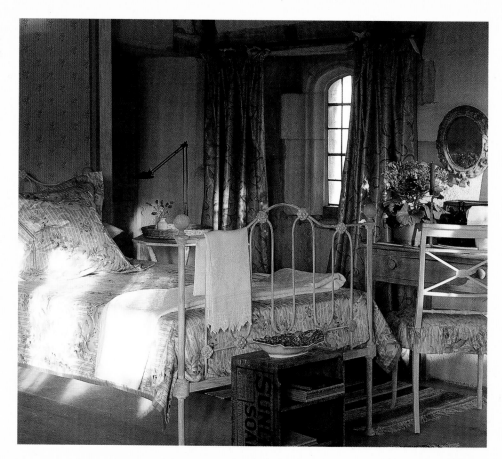

Opposite below

This bedroom is used as an artist's studio. Maximum light has been achieved by allowing the curtains to be drawn to the side of the window; the full window opening is therefore revealed. The curtains are tied at the top to a simple painted pole. The decor is minimal for little distraction, only personal objects and reference books are required, plus brushes, easel and paints. The bed furnishings are of a ticking stripe, which give a tailored crispness to the bed. White smartness and practical comfort detract little from the cast-iron-black painted bedspread. The only concessions to the room's simplicity is the floral decorative screen, geometric rug and embroidered slippers.

Above

Today's Country Style bedrooms combine a subtle combination of old fashion styles with modern convenience and comfort. Many antique beds, with gleaming brass knobs and cast-iron frames, are being skilfully reproduced to offer greater flexibility for size, shape and comfort, than their earlier Victorian counterparts. Bedrooms are also much more spacious, lighter and warmer than our early cottage dweller could have experienced. Today's fashion and interior designer can work with enlightened manufacturers to create complete interior looks, with skilful co-ordination of all aspects of the room. Here total harmony has been achieved in the 'Country Diary' design

'Honeysuckle Rose'; curtains, roller blinds, bedwear and cushions, table-cloth and napkins, together with a small floral wallpaper, have created an instant decorated room. But the skill of the designer would not be complete without the correct accessories. Here Victorian lamps used as a side lamp, and with wall brackets, create that Victorian gas-lamp appearance. Pine dressing-table with over mirror and chest of drawers create a cottage mood when matched together with white painted boarded ceiling. Add a colourful woven rug, wicker chair with a draped Victorian embroidered shawl, and the atmosphere is complete, a room redecorated with an authentic flavour of bygone days.

This sumptuously dressed bed with a canopy-top headboard creates an
atmosphere of wealth and opulence. A feeling of medieval England's
romance and chivalry is conveyed by Plantagenet detailing on the
curtain pelmets and canopy top. Pink creates a warmth and lustre used
simply on a plain fabric quilted coverlet, and frilled valance. The pink
is detailed in the chintz co-ordinating fabric used on curtains,
headboard, canopy and bed cushions. Spacious yet restful, a haven for
peaceful repose, and quiet thoughts, yet having that individual stamp
of a room furnished in the grand manor where the personal preferences
have been pampered and indulged to the full.

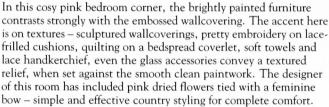

In this cosy pink bedroom corner, the brightly painted furniture contrasts strongly with the embossed wallcovering. The accent here is on textures – sculptured wallcoverings, pretty embroidery on lace-frilled cushions, quilting on a bedspread coverlet, soft towels and lace handkerchief, even the glass accessories convey a textured relief, when set against the smooth clean paintwork. The designer of this room has included pink dried flowers tied with a feminine bow – simple and effective country styling for complete comfort.

Strong pinks and reds with a hint of blue are considered sensuous and voluptuous; pale blush pink on the other hand is pretty and feminine. It is not psychology, but common experience which testifies to the fact that colour above all influences mood and feeling. It certainly is the first consideration when making a decision regarding design or furniture for your room scheme. Pretty pink looks inviting in tungsten light, a candle gives a yellowish pink or peach coloured light. These types of lighting are the most flattering, and the light most people like to see themselves in. Pink is considered a gentle shade, acquiescent and associated with the feminine gender. 'Pink for a girl, blue for a boy' is the traditional saying, but it is based on a logical history. It is not surprising therefore how popular the colour pink is in interior design. Use flatteringly in bedrooms and bathrooms.

Here a pretty pink floral chintz has been used in two scales, large and small, to create a soft delicate feminine mood. The ruffle pillowcases enhance the effect. Soft pink tones are used on woodwork and walls. Pink ceramic accessories complete the dominance and spring flowers create bright accents.

NURSERIES

Above all else a nursery should be colourful and full of interest, not only for learning but to stimulate enquiry and questions, also to add a picturesque content to the room. An assortment of pictures, embroideries, posters and toys conveys a homeliness and safe charm to the child, together with a feeling of belonging, thus establishing roots and security. Here a colonial American look has been achieved. Simple colourful objects and toys haphazardly displayed with an informal cluttered air. The overall effect is one of richness and strength, and is uncompromisingly colonial in inspiration. Patchwork at the turn of the century became less formal in content and design. These colourful fabrics can be used not just as bed-covers, but for throws, table-cloths or as here as a wall hanging and curtains. Samplers convey the colonial atmosphere of the room, but are also ideal amateur works of art to display in a nursery, for they all convey a story and all children love to hear and see stories.

Nurseries should be pretty, practical and yet comfortable. As children grow older they will want to choose a fashionable decorative scheme which usually makes a bold statement about themselves. During the early years, however, the child's room is often an exercise in self-indulgence on the part of the mother. This nursery in blue and pink fairy wallpaper is a complete fanciful indulgence. It is pretty, romantic and practical; everything is at hand and everything is in its place. The delightful fabric is repeated in both the wallpaper and the curtains and accessories include matching cushions and table-cloth. The crisp white bed linen is mirrored in the white shawl which is used as a table throw. Pink and blue toys and paintwork create complementary shades which are repeated in the ceramics, ribbons and bows.

Children's rooms usually have to serve many purposes: that of bedroom, playroom and workroom. They should also be adaptable and grow with the child and change as they change ideas and interest. Surfaces should be tough and practical, to withstand upsets and knocks. But they should be decorated in bright colours, to please the childish eye and stimulate awareness. Space for toys, clothes, books and games, storage (you can never have enough) is vitally important. Dressing-table, wardrobes, chests, drawers or a blanket chest for toys and games are a good idea. The room should not, however, be allowed to become untidy. Discipline begins early, and harmony can be achieved if common colours, here yellow and white, create order, control and a simple unity to the room. Paintwork on walls, doors and wardrobes, gives practical easy-clean surfaces. A high frieze that cannot be reached by prying hands, and colourful removable covers on chairs in case of accidents or spills, are nice decorative touches. A small shelf for special friends and toys but out of reach to selection and return completes the effect – everything in its place and a place for everything.

GARDEN ROOMS

A conservatory can consist of almost any enclosed area built on to the side of your home, which can then be treated as a traditional comfortable space for relaxing and dining, available in all seasons and in all weathers. It is a special place where house and garden meet, creating a bridge between the outside world and your private rooms. Many department stores also stock a wide variety of appropriate furniture, reflecting the current revival of interest in bamboo, cane, wicker and wood as well as traditional cast-iron reproduction furniture. With a little searching around builder's yards or antique shops, many an old original ornamental piece can be found or old container adapted to a new use. Novelty can be a charming asset. Remember that wood, wicker and rattan furniture need protection from strong sunlight. To prevent drying or cracking, it is best to apply a coat of varnish or paint to match your overall colour scheme. For upholstery, many designers recommend sturdy canvas, for its practical toughness, in light colours that are less prone to fading. Other fabrics can be used, for instance plasticized fabrics or laminated fabrics are best on outdoor upholstery, as these are both practical, decorative and shower proof. If cushions are made of curtain furnishing material then it is best to take them indoors when not in use, to avoid fading and soiling through dampness. Sound foundations are required if you are planning a conservatory. A good size measures about 2.5m x 3.5m (8ft x 12ft), and many manufacturers make excellent prefabricated styles, from reproduction Victorian glass houses, to simple lean-to extensions. Critical to any conservatory is proper window and door treatments, because these units are exposed to all the elements, rain as well as strong sunlight, so you will need a degree of control not only over ventilation but also shading using blinds or window shades. If used at night window blinds will be necessary to preserve privacy. Canvas or heavyweight cotton is ideal for this purpose.

Above and right

In Victorian times the conservatory was put to purely practical use – the rearing and nurturing of plants and flowers. The potential for using the garden room as an extension of the house went largely unrecognized. Today, however, the true value of a conservatory, whatever its size and shape, has been realized and exploited to the full. The English climate is well known for its volatility – perhaps the one thing we can guarantee is that the sun never shines as much as we would like. Conservatories, therefore, are a boon. Garden rooms, as the name implies, are a happy combination of mixing interior comfort with exterior beauty. Casting caution to the wind, one can choose exotic furniture and fabrics – wicker, rattan, marble, glass and bold oriental prints work particularly well in light, airy conservatories where a preponderance of glass gives added warmth. The addition of central heating will create an extra room that can be used for dining, entertaining, or simply for contemplation, the year round. One is also at liberty to import exotic plants – some of which will grow to considerable height – which mix perfectly with the slightly off-beat furniture. Other suitable accessories include trellises for colourful climbers, hanging pots and baskets and ethnic jardinières of various sizes – all of which can provide a profusion of colour in your garden room.

Opposite

A gazebo or sleeping porch, as they are sometimes called, is a romantic, cosy adjunct to a home, either situated in the garden or attached to the house. Although the basic construction is similar, you can quite soon personalize them to suit your own interest and style. Window seats, as here, can create additional storage in a small space, and fitted flat cushions are useful for cleaning and easy maintenance. Scatter cushions are comfortable for sitting or lounging in a relaxed mood.

SUMMER

Flower Show

SUMMER

' The evening comes, the fields are still,
The tinkle of the thirsty rill
Unheard all day ascends again;
Deserted is the half-mown plain,
Silent the swathes! the ringing wain,
The mower's cry, the dogs alarms,
All housed within the sleeping farms!
The business of the day is done,
The last-left hay-maker is gone.
And from the thyme upon the height,
And from the elder-blossom white
And pale dog-roses in the hedge,
And from the mint plant in the sedge,
In puffs of balm the night-air blows
The perfume which the day fore-goes.
And on the pure horizon far,
See, pulsing with the first-born star,
The liquid sky above the hill!
The evening comes, the fields are still. '

Matthew Arnold.

The warmth of the sun, the lazy, hazy days filled with the scent of honeysuckle, rose, lavender and May blossom – these are the tangible pleasures of summer. The flowers, both wild and cultivated, which bring colour and sweet scents to the countryside, create a multicoloured palette in full profusion – the bright pinks, reds, blues, the mixing of warm tints with clean greens, browns and natural greys.

Opposite and right
Entrances and hallways are transient areas of the home, as you proceed through them to somewhere else. This does not, however, betoken that they are unimportant in their ranking for decorative attention – they are a home's introduction, a staging post from welcome to hospitality. They are also a functional area – for arrivals and departures, and although these encounters will not suffer unduly with longevity they should be pleasurable.

If windows are the eyes of a home, then the doorway must service as its mouth and as windows as passive, doors and entrance areas are a hive of activity. These areas usually contain a certain amount of personal clutter – and if a porchway is attached, this can be a depositary for shoes, wellingtons, cloaks, scarves and umbrellas, together with the occasional package, basket/ shopping bag, or newspaper and post until claimed and sorted. Doors, halls and entrances therefore are our personal frontier posts allowing the outside into the inside and beckoning us to a haven of comfort and friendliness. They provide us with a retreat from an ever demanding world – doorways admit surprises and delights, fresh air, tearful farewells or joyous renunions. They are our point of contact between our private and public worlds and hallways are our access from one world to another, whether we are retreating, arriving, departing or returning.

Left
Country decorating does not follow a strict set of rules. Instead it is based on an eclectic practical approach that incorporates a variety of different solutions. It will change with the seasons, as much as the food you prepare and the way you wish to eat it. Either formal dining with the wine chilled and candles lit, places set and laid and guests escorted to defined positions (to assist good conversation and discussion); or fast, friendly and informal as a piece of toast, muffins, tea, jam and scones, eaten in your lap, curled up with a good book or crossword or while listening to the radio. Everyone's idea of a summer cottage is epitomized in this charming kitchen, simply bursting with sunlight and fresh flowers. White walls again create the maximum feeling of spaciousness. 'Country Diary' table and kitchen linens, plus the close proximity to the garden terrace help to bridge the barrier between the garden and the house to create a kitchen with the essential smells and colours of the countryside.

Left
In this sunny kitchen white not only cleans and refreshes but allows kitchen clutter to become the focus. The pretty 'Country Diary' collection designs as shown on the table-cloth, kitchen cloths and ceramics, brings the summer freshness of flowers into the kitchen. Country objects abound and dried flowers, herbs and baskets, crocks, pots and containers litter the shelves and window-sills, each surface begging for a collection of objects which create country charm and atmosphere.

Opposite
Wood, brick, plaster and tile used here in roof timbers, ceilings, walls and flooring, create the basic foundation for country architecture. Simple, sparse, practical and functional, natural materials reflect natural living. This kitchen is a far cry from its medieval ancestors – fitted units in country pine give ample work surfaces between equipment. Good lighting is also very important as illustrated here.

Natural surfaces achieved here on wooden doors, window casements, cupboards and flooring, either left plain, waxed or varnished, create the rustic idyll of the scrubbed, bleached table top of grandma's kitchen, but really suggest an uncluttered caring for simplicity in style. Here this kitchen/dining-room, that connects to a morning-room, allows the summer sunlight to illuminate the proud origins of simple country comforts, modest yet correct in an understated style. Plain white lace window drapes allow maximum natural daylight to fill the high-ceilinged rooms with the fresh airiness of the country. Clean, crisp linens cover the table top with a plainness that offsets the bright colour contrast of fresh fruit in a white bowl. The room is complete; it needs nothing more.

The cottage industry of cooking must have been made less of a chore, when things were at hand, and there was a place for everything and everything in its place. The country kitchen was usually as personalized and customized as a 'formula one' racing car today. The cook of yesterday filled her kitchen with practical objects, and as space was usually at a premium, this evoked a feeling of country clutter, which has since spread to all parts of our homes, conveying a decorative profusion of objects and patterns that are the hallmark of Country Style's practicality. In a cottage setting knick-knacks abound, groups of objects mostly practical (but some can be purely decorative) look perfect on walls, shelves or dressers. Shelves invite collections of bric-a-brac and plates of all shapes and sizes, and patterns – as bright and colourful as a summer's garden.

SUMMERTIME BLUES

Opposite above; below, left and right
Blue and white transfer-printed earthenware was produced in vast quantities in the early nineteenth century. It was made mainly in the district known as the Staffordshire Potteries but also in Yorkshire, Lancashire, Northumberland and South Wales. Many people collect it avidly and the pleasure and interest derived from the thousands of different patterns produced is remarkable. But as blue is the most universally popular colour, perhaps it is not so surprising. Series of blue-printed wares were produced showing views of castles, ruins and river scenery. Town and cities were featured or historical events commemorated. These can all be sought out and found by the collector.

The first earthenwares to be transfer-printed in blue and then glazed were produced in 1780 by Thomas Turner at Caughley in Shropshire. This new style of decoration was to have a dramatic effect on the pottery industry. Early years were experimental and most patterns were derived from Chinese ceramics. With the development of paper-printing techniques, rapid advances were made and finer engravings produced remarkable richness and quality. Many of the plates and dishes had borders of garden flowers or scenes of country life. Many patterns echoed contemporary designs on fabrics and wallpapers. Their popularity has continued and today many kitchen dressers, drawing-rooms or window-sills display a fine collection, or perhaps an individual jug filled with flowers.

Above
It was not only the Potteries that found such a prolific use for the indigo blue colour. Rich calico cotton has for centuries been individually decorated with blue designs. Indigo caught the imagination of the Western world during the early sixteenth century when traders returned home with the riches of India and the Far East. The design and pattern produced by today's manufacturers have changed little in style from their eighteenth-century counterparts. Calicos have that homespun appeal; reproductions of chintz and woven coverlets give a feeling of freshness on clean crisp white cotton or cream base cloth and add a sparkle of eastern spice to any interior.

Through the technical advances in copper-plate printing, others were making full use of Indigo prints. Christopher Philippe Oberkamp, of Jouy in France, was producing fabrics quite stunning in quality, with inspirations from oriental, pictorial scenes, classical ruins and printed floral motifs – these fine goods again found an eager market in both American and European cultures, proving the universal popularity of the colour. These *Toiles-de-Jouy* prints are still fashionable today and have recently gained a new vogue in styling awareness – today we live in a century distant from the vast plantations of India, in a world surrounded by colours of every imaginable hue and shade. Yet in spite of this wealth of colour, indigo retains a place unique and special – the dominant place in colour popularity. Blue has travelled far from the Mogul emperors through fabric and fashion, from Java's prints to Levi jeans, it continues to maintain its enhancing attraction in our homes and interiors.

Above
A pale pine floor and an abundance of rustic basketry complement
the mellow colours of the Country Diary 'Springtime' design on the
wallpapers and textiles in this light and well-styled room.

Opposite
In almost any decorative design scheme wallpaper is a quick and
inexpensive way to create the correct mood and style. However, in
a small space with many light switches, cupboards, obstacles, plus
acute corners and angles, it may be better to leave it to a
professional to produce the desired effect. Many wallpapers
available today have special water-resistant finishes that increase
their strength and practicality. Here vinyl wallpaper has been used
in a shower area, and this small floral print brings summer freshness
to the room. Co-ordinated shower curtains, bathroom curtains, tie-
backs, light shade, embroidered towels and ceramics, provide a
unity which is simple to achieve. Brass taps, shower fittings, rails
and mirror provide a light sparkle to soften the heavy Victorian
bathroom fixtures.

By the early twentieth century bathing and washing facilities were extensive as the new industrial wealth developed. A 'new rich' middle-class society was eager to emulate the landed gentry. Baths were free standing or wooden framed. Showers existed, but were not very popular with the Victorians. They consisted of a circular curtain in the centre of the bath, with a shower head above, or three sided, placed at one end of the bath. Most basins were heavy structures, set in a wooden cabinet, with tiled splashback, flanked by gas lights and set with an oval or circular mirror for grooming. Foot baths were also available, usually combined with a seat for safe bathing. As the twentieth century wore on, and after two world wars, which brought a more practical utilitarianism to domestic life, the bathroom became much less the furnished room our Victorian ancestors had enjoyed. It became a practical tiled shell with fittings and plumbing confined to one wall, a far cry from the middle-class Victorian bathroom with all its space and trimmings.

This visually strong Victorian-style bathroom is surprisingly unified by using only blue and white as a decorative theme. The scenic toile wallpaper forms an intricate background for eclectic clutter of blue and white ceramics and romantic prints. Though highly decorative, the two wall-shelf units can provide a practical answer for the storage of soaps, salts, pot-pourri, as well as other accessories. A heavy embossed wallpaper has been over-painted a rich deep blue to give surface interest and a plain contrast to a busy wallpaper. This also helps highlight the beautiful shapes of well-designed sanitary ware. Simple white pedestal basin, bidet, claw-footed, free-standing bath and the old-style toilet cistern look perfectly in character. Brass fitments and fittings – taps, towel rail and pipe work – complete the traditional feeling. Stripped pine flooring, white paint work and a scrubble washed ceiling reinforce the feeling without competing for visual attention, while the highlight stencil feature on the old tub shows how details can be all important. Details have been considered further by using a blue ribbon bow to support Victorian prints, pretty frilled curtains and decoration bathroom rug with 'bluebird' motifs.

COUNTRY CLUTTER

An intriguing mixture of cluttered shelves contrasts sharply against white walls and a plain ticking-stripe sofa, or does it? Harmony has been created by a dominance of white which sparkles from ceramics, fabrics or walls, all differing in surface texture, so the subtle changes create a feeling of harmony more than contrast. This room is typical of many of today's bedsit or multi-purpose rooms: the emphasis is on traditional values and personal clutter. Pine dresser and wicker furnishings have been combined with modern upholstery and contemporary prints. Furniture and antiques create a comfortable ambience as distinctive and individual as a finger print. A splash of dried flowers displayed in a country basket is in natural harmony with profusions of fresh plants in a variety of tubs, pots and bowls. Comfort without pretensions is the hallmark of English Country Style. The mixture and blending of decorative ingredients can therefore be an intriguing mixture of plain and fancy components.

With a strong statement in paintwork – here flame red has been used to anchor collective clutter to make a bold statement in style. It matters not what each individual item of interest is in the room, as the dominant feature is the colour of the room. This over emphasis creates unity out of chaos and order from an undisciplined collection of objects.

Traditional 'chintz' prints create a country house harmony. Beautiful colourful fabrics exude comfort and elegance. Cushions layered for comfort and support create a relaxed mood by their informality. The atmosphere supports good conversation and enjoyment for family and friends. A pretty floral, striped chintz covers the little sofa, curtains are pleated on to a simple wooden pole in a co-ordinating coloured stripe. An ornate wrought-iron wall light supports candles. Small antique objects are cluttered with country objects, plants and fresh flowers. A small display case contains ceramics and objects displayed with a common thread – jugs, cups, saucers and plates – but quite unrelated objects can be grouped together and can still manage to look cohesive and interesting. Country Style contains no clearly defined rules, which means plenty of scope for imaginative experimentation. Colours do, however, create a feeling of harmony, and large rooms can happily accommodate several fabrics or designs; these can be united by a common colour theme. But a small room like this looks best when the decoration is more restrained and built around a single idea or colour.

FLOWERING OF CHINTZ

Opposite and above

Nothing conveys English Country Style more than the traditional elegance of chintz. It is the most symbolic of all things English, making living-rooms both luxurious and liveable. Chintz fabrics combine that subtle richness of colour, with a feeling of traditional quality and comfort. These rich multicoloured designs, of cascading flowers, ribbons, swags and oriental blossoms, birds and landscapes, blend into any interior. Like a chameleon adapts its colouring to fit its surroundings so does the chintz fabric blend comfortably into most homes. Chintz comes from the Hindu word *chint* meaning spotted or having variation, but today it has come to mean glazed cotton fabric, visually attractive and practical, as the glaze improves wear and resists dirt. These designs first appeared in Europe in the early seventeenth century with the expansion of the Indo-European textile trade. Their popularity is still maintained centuries later, which indicates their lasting properties of both styling and use. Today, authentic English chintz may be identified by deep and subtle colours, richly tasselled and trimmed, still with a grand proliferation of flowers, birds in oriental shades, brought together in living-room, dining-room, bedroom or bathroom, bringing romance, elegant comfort and country charm to interiors.

The charm of the elegance of English style and the charm of the eighteenth century has been successfully transplanted into this drawing-room. Awash with bright sunlight, the strong jewel-tone colours of the rich tapestry table-cloth, upholstery and window furnishings convey a careful blending of patterns and colours – featuring several patterns of chintzed fabrics. These are complemented by striking plain-coloured upholstery, and a richness of eclectic clutter. A careful attention to detail is reflected by the blue and white ceramic lamps, and the display cabinet of decorative plates, period oil paintings, together with shell flowers and a dome. Even the variety of floor treatments, from carpet, quarry tiles, rush matting and floor-boards, creates a structural division to separate the different room functions, from dining, writing, relaxing or just passing through.

Above
A great slab of stonework, whitewashed white for lightness and freshness, conveys a time-worn elegance, of simple country farmhouse comforts with that 'lived in' appeal. This room seems to have gradually evolved rather than been decoratively created. Furniture has been positioned for use rather than for appearance. Furniture that you can sink into after a hard day's work. A room of simple tastes, simply displayed.

Right
The medieval hall of the fifteenth century which was used as the main dining area, was covered in rush or straw. Hangings covering the walls and hung 'as if in a church' – the latter having been previously the only place where such decorations had been seen. The custom of painting walls, which had been general under Henry III, declined gradually, and its place was taken by hangings of tapestry. Popular motifs were leopards of gold, falcons, swans, stars, birds, griffins, eagles and flowers to mention but a few. Heraldic tapestries were also popular means of indicating lineage and rank. Although the furniture remained primitive – benches and trestled tables with a high dias for nobility – eating and drinking were considered to have reached an advanced stage. The high-table was covered with a linen cloth and the platters were of pewter, with squares of wood for the servants. At the king's table, silver or even gold plate was used. The use of glass for drinking vessels was rare but not unknown; glass cups were imported from Venice and were looked upon as precious possessions, more common materials were horn and earthenware.

The dining area for an open-plan interior needs to reflect upon, and perhaps co-ordinate with, the adjacent living-room in terms of colour scheme, style of furnishings, wallpaper, floor treatment and upholstery. In a separate dining-room you obviously have more scope to create a more individual solution, but even here it is better to create a solution that complements that of adjacent rooms of the individual house style. Despite the evolution of dining-room design, the function remains consistent, as does the furniture: table, (round, oval or oblong); chairs; sideboard to assist in the serving of drinks and food, also for storage of linen, cutlery and drinks; display cabinet for glass, china and delicate objects of mainly decorative use. With these rather simple items of functional furniture to accommodate, it is through the style and decor – colour and furnishings – that mood and individuality will be communicated. Perhaps this mood is conveyed through the delicate pale shades of the Regency period, or the heavy fabric drapes and busy dark

wallpapers of the Victorian period. Is it light and contemporary or traditional? Country comfort (with pine and place mats) or romantic with lace table-cloth on an oak table with high-backed windsor chairs – the decision is yours.

The dining-room is most likely the best place in which to indulge in beautiful table accessories. The best dinner service, cut-glass decanters and glass of Waterford crystal, place settings with fine cutlery and embroidered napkins or plain-coloured linen. The visual impact of old silver, silver-plate serving pieces or candle-sticks on a polished table top is unforgettable. Antique shops, house sales and market bric-a-brac stalls can be good sources for these items, or you may already have a family collection of household linens and table accessories that have been passed on to you from past generations. All these can be displayed at the right time in the right way to give pleasure and highlight the occasion.

Left and below
These rooms reflect the abundance of summer flowers, whether decoratively featured or on wallcoverings or bed-linen fabrics, the impact of blossoms and blooms, sprays and flowers stimulate a particular richness, due to their multicoloured profusion of patterns. Choose a light colour to complement their dominance in the room. To create a harmony, investigate light pastel versions of the rich highlighted colours – pinks, blues, sea green or beige. These colours will provide a soft background and allow the fabric and wallpapers to take on a 'custom look'. Varied ceiling treatments, using wallpapers of different pattern densities, can create decorative features of alcoves, but the rest of the furnishings should be simple and organized into neat accents to avoid chaos. Another suitable alternative might be simple white walls and minimal clutter to offset the abundance of blossoms.

Nothing enhances a romantically designed bedroom like heavy frills and an abundance of drapery. Rich colours and heavy floral bouquets are pleasantly complemented by a dainty patterned wallpaper and frieze. The window treatments give a grandeur to the room, by adding extra length to the drapes and creating, when drawn, a wall of fabric to add to the feeling of richness. The pelmet swags have been deeply ruched and finished off in the centre with a false bow in matching fabric. The duvet cover continues this theme by using the same floral pattern, but a co-ordinating small print is used on the reverse side of the duvet, fitted sheet, valance, lamp shade and cushions. Frills have been added to the duvet and pillowcases to create the overall effect. The botanical feel is further developed by filling the fireplace with baskets of dried flowers and plants. Fresh flowers decorate the mantelpiece and dressing table, giving a summer fragrance to the room. Botanical framed prints decorate the wall above the bed, and small woven posies are highlighted in the bedside rug. The floral sophistication of the room is not disturbed by the casual discarding of summer hats, shawl and picnic basket. This predominant feeling of floral richness is successfully offset by the cream-painted ceiling, door and mantelpiece, plain simple bedside lamps and a plain self-coloured carpet.

Country decorating is much more formal in England than in America as these examples clearly show. The bed is transformed to become a simple decorative shape, to feature soft delicate flowers in panel and border treatments, with delicate summer flowers scattered and tossed in trails or bouquets, on pillows, duvets and curtains. These provide a tranquillity of styling that creates a softness to allow a plethora of accessories to highlight the rooms. Stain glass creates a medieval feature, recreating a romantic mood of the Victorian art and crafts movement. Simple jug and bowl, wash stand, botanical prints, ceramics, decoy ducks, plus natural plants and summer flowers complete the scene. The planked flooring either painted or stripped, together with primitive rugs, reinforce the essence of country styling. Whether in essence America or English the rustic feeling of 'Country' anchors these bedrooms, and sets the tone for summer sunlight to create the warmth.

Country romance is a life-style built on friendliness and informality and is not as remote from day-to-day living as the novelists would have you believe. Romance is enhanced by the creation of the right atmosphere in a room, using colours and designs that have sympathy with each other and truly reflect your mood. They define spaciousness or confinement, indicated use or function (for instance you would not paint your kitchen the same colour as your bedroom) colours also suggest warmth or coldness. The right choice will undoubtedly influence your mood and project your personality – your rooms will suggest much that is true about yourself. This is an important factor in interior design, as you live in the room, so it should reflect your character.

Lace can create a Victorian homespun atmosphere. Antique lace is often quite inexpensive and is sold by many shops. Table runners and napkins, in normally off-white shades, give a traditional period warmth. Good-quality new lace is still manufactured and 'Nottingham lace' is still available, as extensive ranges are frequently introduced. Appliqués, hand-painted fabrics and embroidered table-clothes make lovely gifts. The table setting can be completed by a flower arrangement; this can be of natural flowers that reflect the season's colours, or silk artificial flowers and nature's dried-flower beauty.

For most people who wish to create this comfortable room, decorating can be the ultimate challenge, yet tempered by compromise. One rarely makes a fresh start from bare walls or plaster, and an empty space can be a daunting prospect. There will usually exist a main item of furniture – bed, dresser or side table – a favourite print or painting, or perhaps an existing carpet to consider. Country romance reflects this mixture of inherited values from either treasured heirlooms or basic functional items, to new furnishings, colours or changes in fashions, room occupation and use. Everything in a room makes a statement and colour is the most important. The main features (or elements) are paint, wallpaper, carpets, curtains, lamp shades and rugs, as these can be more flexible in their use. Therefore, changing fashions and greater choice of variety should be reflected mainly by changes of colour in accentuating items in your room. For furniture, floor and wallcoverings, constitute considerable investments which once made will endure, to create that well-lived-in comfortable room.

CREATIVE WALLS

Opposite, above and below
In this room the designer has created a mix-and-match opportunity by subtle changes in scale and layout; large all-over prints are ideal for co-ordination at windows. The larger floral has been used for a full rich curtain and plain net for a festoon blind. The main floral print has been adapted on the frilled duvet and frilled pillowcases and fitted valance sheet. The small floral co-ordinates on the wallpaper. The frieze is an adaptation of the two elements to add direction by means of a border trail. The rich blossoms produce a feeling of comfortable luxury. The natural foliage of fresh bright flowers or a dried bouquet makes the room a personal retreat, for sleep, to enjoy a good book, or to write that letter or to sit up and await the tray of morning tea. This is English Country Style at its most gracious.

Right, above and below
Wall colours are important, and paint is not the sole product to use, although extensive in shades and varied in finish. Wallpapers and borders can quite easily and inexpensively evoke the correct mood and style, providing a simple and effective solution only if your walls and plasterwork are sound. Fabric draped on rods spanning the length of the room is a more exotic approach, but creates a really romantic look and hides walls that perhaps are in less than good condition. To create that authentic country charm and flavour, the finished surface brickwork, natural or painted white, is still the best solution. Grooved pine stripped or stencilled is a suitable alternative. Polished oak panels give walls a quality of timeless heritage. Stone, slate or simple white plasterwork create country cottage quality.

Your room might reflect the English country cottage of sound domestic sturdiness, with your furnishings emanating from their simple homespun charms (for rural style is not only locked in the past, but transcends and adapts so well with high-tech efficiency) or it may reflect the grace and splendour of the English country house (classical in feeling and gracious in restraint). Or perhaps it is a hybrid of these two styles that mixes new and old in a contemporary arrangement of collective clutter. One thing is certain that whatever the ingredients, the style will be in the mixture, and the match will suit your room and your personality and reflect English country flavours at their most tasty.

POTS AND PLANTS

Above, left and right

If you have a large garden then you are fortunate, but a smaller plot can still be a joy to behold in terms of colour, style and fragrance. However, a modest outdoor verandah, deck or simply screened porch can still be a delight. Beautiful miniature gardens can be created on flat roofs, balconies or even in a modest window-box. You can create that outdoor feeling, or fill your interior with bright summer flowers, herbs or small shrubs, and with the aid of tubs and containers you can add a splash of colour to your terrace or room. I remember visiting my grandfather's gloriously overgrown garden,

when a small child. There was a path leading to a secluded rose arbour, where the scent of the flowers was wonderful; in the centre was an enormous classical Grecian urn on a pedestal base. The flowering plants inside cascaded over the rim, petals fell around its base, and moss covered the stem. It was always my favourite place in the garden, and most memorable. This feature, and many similar, can be easily emulated today, now that so many attractive containers are available for outdoor plants from supermarkets, chain stores and garden centres. Wooden tubs, urns, terracotta pots and stone troughs filled with flowers, will provide attractive colour accents to highlight a corner of a garden or on a terrace or patio. There are also the traditional half-round log tubs in larch, oriental glazed Chinese pots for bulbs or ferns, old, discarded wheelbarrows and tanks, and the old faithful half wooden barrel. All these and many more than can be illustrated here, when filled with bulbs, flowers, or herbs, will provide attractive colour and foliage, and with a little ingenuity create a spectacular display, when mixed and clustered on door step, patio, window ledge or terrace.

Left

Reconstituted limestone can be made into some most beautiful shapes like this fluted and leaf-decorated vase. It is ideal for walkways or as a centre feature on a patio. These superb reproductions of classical urns, bowls, vases and jardinières (opposite) have a Portland Stone appearance and texture, to bring a classical seventeenth-century quality to your display of plants. However, these items are quite expensive; cheaper and equally attractive are terracotta pots, with classical embellishments of ribbons, leaves, lions or cherubs. Terracotta is water absorbent and benefits growth. These pots are perfect for any location.

Chiselled from blocks of York stone, these ornamental troughs are heavy, but practical, and convey a country crafted look. Ideal for alpines, bulbs, summer bedding and many other plants, they have a solid, ageless beauty. Because of their weight these planters virtually become permanent features in your garden. They all have drainage holes, and are usually frost resistant.

POTS AND PLANTS

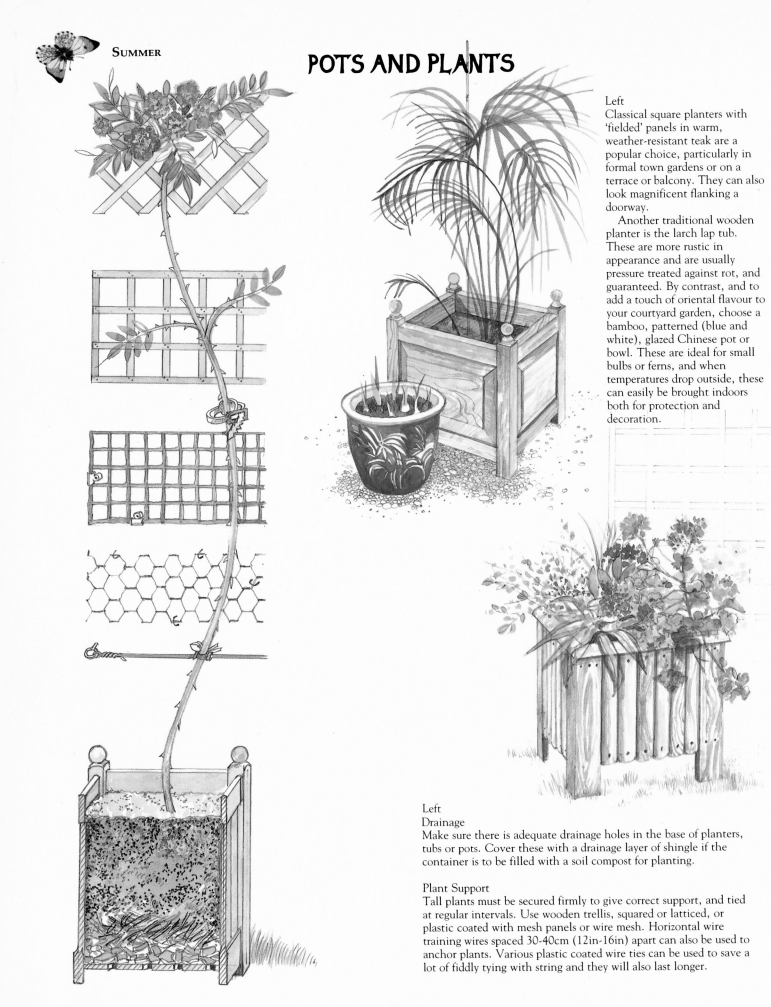

Left
Classical square planters with 'fielded' panels in warm, weather-resistant teak are a popular choice, particularly in formal town gardens or on a terrace or balcony. They can also look magnificent flanking a doorway.

Another traditional wooden planter is the larch lap tub. These are more rustic in appearance and are usually pressure treated against rot, and guaranteed. By contrast, and to add a touch of oriental flavour to your courtyard garden, choose a bamboo, patterned (blue and white), glazed Chinese pot or bowl. These are ideal for small bulbs or ferns, and when temperatures drop outside, these can easily be brought indoors both for protection and decoration.

Left
Drainage
Make sure there is adequate drainage holes in the base of planters, tubs or pots. Cover these with a drainage layer of shingle if the container is to be filled with a soil compost for planting.

Plant Support
Tall plants must be secured firmly to give correct support, and tied at regular intervals. Use wooden trellis, squared or latticed, or plastic coated with mesh panels or wire mesh. Horizontal wire training wires spaced 30-40cm (12in-16in) apart can also be used to anchor plants. Various plastic coated wire ties can be used to save a lot of fiddly tying with string and they will also last longer.

Hanging Baskets and Window Boxes (below)
To make maintenance easier, suspend high hanging baskets from a device that allows them to be lowered to a working level for trimming, tidying and watering. Imaginatively planted with gay summer flowers, hanging baskets will brighten a porch or patio for many months of the year. Window boxes can be secured in place with a length of wire run between two vine eyes, one either side, screwed to the wall. As a general rule, avoid obvious contrasts, choosing plants that provide an harmonious effect. The overall appearance can be enhanced by trailing plants.

Permanent Plants (above)
Using large containers like half oak barrels or cast concrete bowls, large perennial plants can be used with small pots, boxes and bowls, to create a more mature patio or deck. However, these will need lots of watering (particularly during the summer months) because of the limited rooting space.

Terrarium (right)
Use any fairly large clear glass container to make a terrarium or bottle garden, such as an old carboy, fish tank or one of the attractive purpose-made ones that are widely available from any good garden centre. Some plants that are difficult to grow in the drier air of a sitting-room thrive in these more humid conditions.

85

FIRST PRIZE

AUTUMN

BOTTLE FRUITS.
Apples
Apricots
Blackberries
Cherries
Cranberries
Currants Black
Currants Red
Damsons
Rhubarb

AUTUMN

To Autumn.

Season of mists and mellow fruitfulness!
  Close bosom-friend of the maturing sun;
  Conspiring with him how to load and bless
With fruit the vines that round the thatch-eaves run;
  To bend with apples the moss'd cottage-trees,
    And fill all fruit with ripeness to the core;
  To swell the gourd and plump the hazel shells
    With a sweet kernel; to set budding more,
  And still more, later flowers for the bees,
  Until they think warm days will never cease,
  For Summer has o'er-brimmed their clammy cells.

Who hath not seen thee oft amid thy store?
  Sometimes whoever seeks abroad may find
Thee sitting careless on a granary floor,
  Thy hair soft-lifted by the winnowing wind;
Or on a half-reap'd furrow sound asleep,
Drowsed with the fume of poppies while thy hook
  Spares the next swathe and all its twined flowers;
And sometimes like a gleaner thou dost keep
  Steady thy laden head across a brook;
  Or by a cider-press, with patient look,
Thou watchest the last oozings hours by hours.

                                        J. Keats

Autumn is golden leaves, fruit berries and heathers in bloom; ripe corn colours rich in hue, deep in shade; warm bright days with strong warm breezes; poppies red amidst the gold of corn and fawn of grasses; country walks down lanes covered with harebells. The berries on trees and bushes are beginning to make themselves conspicuous, and time is spent collecting flowers for drying and for creating permanent displays that bring the exquisite beauty of the countryside into living-rooms, kitchens and parlours.

Above

The hallway has always been an eminently practical space of great value. It's where you drop your shopping, parcels, post, hats and umbrella; it also stores overcoats, raincoats, boots and shoes. At the same time the entrance or hallway is the first impression a visiting guest or visiting neighbour will have of the house style and it will reflect your personality and set the tone for the entire house.

With all this activity and scrutiny, chatter, and commotion it is not an area of the home in which we spend much time, but its effect on others is considerable. The first and most important consideration in decorating your hallway is its size, small areas will need to be made to appear larger by use of little clutter and fresh light paintwork, whereas large expanses of height or area will afford the opportunity for decorative experimentation and statement.

Left

Hallways should reflect the style and interests of the home owner, and the space, though mostly utilitarian by nature, should still provide the backdrop to allow for personal idiosyncrasy in the way the walls are decorated with objects and pictures. Collections of prints or family photographs and curios whether different in shape or subject can make a handsome juxtaposition that makes a house memorable. Eclectic clutter on shelves, window-sills and table top, give life and substance to all rooms. But hallways provide a private glimpse of the personal tastes within a home; they should tempt the taste buds of the visitor and give assurance to the owner either when returning from holiday, or a trip to the shops. Window-sills and hallways can become spaces for flower displays and plants.

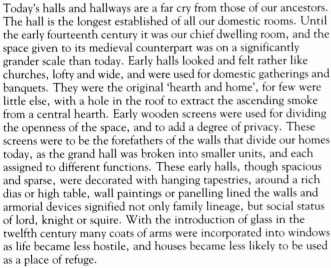

Today's halls and hallways are a far cry from those of our ancestors. The hall is the longest established of all our domestic rooms. Until the early fourteenth century it was our chief dwelling room, and the space given to its medieval counterpart was on a significantly grander scale than today. Early halls looked and felt rather like churches, lofty and wide, and were used for domestic gatherings and banquets. They were the original 'hearth and home', for few were little else, with a hole in the roof to extract the ascending smoke from a central hearth. Early wooden screens were used for dividing the openness of the space, and to add a degree of privacy. These screens were to be the forefathers of the walls that divide our homes today, as the grand hall was broken into smaller units, and each assigned to different functions. These early halls, though spacious and sparse, were decorated with hanging tapestries, around a rich dias or high table, wall paintings or panelling lined the walls and armorial devices signified not only family lineage, but social status of lord, knight or squire. With the introduction of glass in the twelfth century many coats of arms were incorporated into windows as life became less hostile, and houses became less likely to be used as a place of refuge.

The hallway today is a more practical size and its furniture will depend much more on its functional aspects. Many people find a degree of privacy in their hallways, and because of this need it is an ideal place for the telephone unless you can afford numerous extensions. A hall phone allows for a quiet reply without the need to turn down the television or shout for the children's silence. So a chair and side table or desk are ideal starts, in considering functional furniture that is large enough to accommodate the telephone book, message pads, parcels, magazines, or lists and letters. A hall stand for cloaks, umbrellas and shopping bags, hats, scarves and school satchel is also ideal. To allow for free-flowing traffic, especially in a family home, location of any furniture should not restrict movement within the hall area, and permit that unexpected visitor to arrive while you are engaged on the phone. The hallway is also an ideal location for an English long-case grandfather clock or wall clock; it provides a decorative feature in a restricted area.

Left

It is important that you select a theme to establish the look, and focus your ideas in selecting colours and wallpapers. Will it be plain cottage simplicity, or Victorian cheerful clutter, with shelves full of imaginative odds and ends. Establish your priorities, decide what things are important to you, and what you wish to change, or give up. Now is the time to fit more electrical points, or get rid of that old fridge or cupboard. Will what you wish to do conflict too much with the authenticity of the house style, or period? Remember to bring out your home's existing charm and not simply impose your urge for simple convenience. It is all a question of balance. Evaluate your existing furniture and appliances and work out a budget. If you decide to have fitted units, expertly fitted by a local firm, do shop around for the best quote, as they do vary considerably on the amount of work content they commit to, or consider sub contracting some of the work yourself, if you have the time. Ask yourself do you really need to replace at all? If things work then leave them, or incorporate them into your new scheme, to suit your changing requirements, be it pine sideboard, or marble slab. Try to think of new uses for old things.

Opposite above and above
When you have made the decision to redecorate your kitchen do not try to do everything in one go. Make a plan, revise it if required, and time each phase, step by step to completion. Also schedule the work in the correct order, to save time and expense. Do not use ready-made plastic laminates in fashionable mixed colours for counter tops. Although practical they will date too quickly and detract from that country feel you are trying to achieve with your restoration. However, self-coloured plastic is alright, as this will not depend on fashion, and used with a wood front edge and a panelled or tiled spashback it will suit your interior much better. Do not overdo authenticity – just because it is old it does not mean it is better. Remember to create the correct balance between traditional values and practical efficiency. Do not use contemporary designed vinyl flooring, the patterns will be out of character and dilute your effect. Better to use wood-block flooring, or tile squares with picket edges to create an interesting floor – or checker-board in two-tone shade with a border pattern, to create a finished outline shape to your room. Quarry tiles, or old flags, make an ideal floor, or brick waxed to a glowing finish gives warmth and harmony to your kitchen. Remember you only do this once so get it right first time. Do not sacrifice convenience unless you have to. After all, your kitchen is a food preparation area and work centre. So do not forget ventilation. Windows stay clear, on fine summer days, but what about the condensation and smells in winter months. Fit an extractor hood above your stove to remove excess steam and cooking odours at source. Also a window fan is ideal for extraction and ventilation, as most now have reverse action and do both jobs.

Kitchens should convey that lived-in comfortable appeal of home-baked mum's apple pie; warmth and country-sweet flavours should be instantly conveyed to the visitor, as here in this kitchen, which is surprisingly busy and cluttered with country fare and flavours. Kitchens are ideal galleries for collections: much-loved baskets, dried herbs, cooking pots and pans, storage jars (for jams and pickles) containers and crocks of every shape and size. Wooden worktops are practical and authentic. The warmth of wood, either on worktop or giant roof beam conveys a strength and tradition of days gone by.

COUNTRY CLUTTER

Above
Today the medieval concept of the 'keeping room' is returning, as the kitchen once more takes centre stage in family life, as all the family now do the kitchen chores. Working mums can leave things in the freezer, timer oven or microwave and bring freshly cooked food to the table.

Right
Consider the resurgent popularity of natural materials – marble and granite, for traditional finished surfaces and a feeling of opulence. Man-made substitutes and simulated materials have improved in authenticity recently, and offer a wider selection than ever at considerably less cost. Here, rustic granite slabs and a motley collection of country tackle set the scene at the kitchen door.

Opposite
Pay attention to floor levels especially when trying to create a flat even work surface. Also think about cabinet door heights. Should they be capped below ceiling or, to gain additional space for storage, be extended to full ceiling height. Also glass doors are popular and convey that old country-cupboard feeling, for china displays and as accents themselves. Consider panelling as a decorative feature on a wall, or below a bar top or work area, adding a cosy rustic feature in country pine. Or perhaps you could find some old oak panels from a builder's yard or recovery merchant. All these will add character to your kitchen. But if this is not your wish then consider old-style wallpapers, colourful collections (as here, bowls and jugs), border prints, or stencilled ceilings, woodwork or walls.

SAMPLERS

Above and opposite
Sampler making tells us much about social, religious and industrial trends. Samplers convey the history of the times in which they were so patiently sewn and executed more than most history books. They show the art and traditions of English life through the gentle craft of embroidery, telling the tale with a touching charm sometimes sad and a little naive in sentiment – in essence the heart of English Country Style. The word sampler comes from the latin *exemplum*, meaning something chosen from a number of things ... an example to be followed. The word was also derived from the old French word *exemplaire* or *essamplaire* and denoting in medieval English any kind of model or pattern to follow, copy or imitate. Samplers are the most recognized early embroideries, and from the early seventeenth century to the mid nineteenth century innumerable small girls in England and English colonies overseas, worked one or more samplers in the course of their strict school-day exercises. The age of these amateur embroideresses was between five and fifteen, copying their tutor's model, under close supervision.

However, the individual could exercise a degree of personal selection with regard to the arrangements of motifs, flowers, birds, plants and homes, all detailed in a variety of stitches and colours. The resulting sampler would be created and treasured as a thing of worth and beauty, possessing considerable talent and childish charm. Not all specimens were the work of children however, some showed the professional touch of the skilled needle woman who devoted her leisure moments to the perfection of this craft. For ornament or display, for apparel or furnishing her home with decorative or functional items from seat cushions to table linen, they were finely executed with personal pride in her finished achievements. It is quite apparent that these early samplers, produced in pleasurable company and conversation, were indispensable to their makers. Their appearance in Britain coincided with the flourishing of domestic embroidery, as ecclesiastical garments declined in their richness and finery.

The sampler was a sentimental object which, having taken months to complete, was cherished by the maker or her family. Such a piece of work would not be lightly discarded, and it is not surprising that today there is a revival in interest. For what began as an educational exercise and social custom has gained increased recognition in its own right as a highly prized collector's item. Cross stitch was the universal favourite stitch, and when the sampler ceased to form part of girl's educational development the skills of the seamstress declined and florentine, rococo, chain, tent and satin, together with back stitch, Algerian and Hungarian ceased to feature in this skilful, painstaking art form.

The decline in the sampler as a form of feminine education died out in the second half of the nineteenth century. Samplers today are worked as a hobby and still record important family or national events. Sampler kits, which are usually sold with the pattern already printed on to the linen or canvas, with a guide to suggest stitches, as well as wool or thread, are becoming increasingly popular. These are generally good for children, but fail to gain the professional's regard as they leave little to stimulate creativity or imagination.

Opposite

A bathroom under the eaves conveys a feeling of cosy cottage security. The world outside seems somehow distant, in a little haven away from the daily toils. Country bathrooms can sometimes be quite sparsely furnished to reflect the simple practical nature of country living. A back-to-basics bathroom can, however, be enhanced with pretty folksy flowered wallpapers and curtains, that truly reflect the season's colours. Autumn poppies create here the warmth and charm of country freshness when used on shower curtains and embroidered towels and matching bath mat. Note the Victorian tub with its claw feet, again a feature to evoke mood and period correctness. Curtain poles have been decorated with country ribbons, to reflect autumn colours. Pictures and country objects can complete the look, but a flagged floor can be both a practical period asset and a finished decorative solution – it can only mellow with time. Wooden towel rails can be easily moved to suit use, or decoratively placed to divide the space.

Above

Flowers and light in the bathroom evoke that country manor house feeling of the grand room. Autumn sunlight shines at a low angle, and can turn your early morning refreshing bath into an awakening experience. Here pretty floral curtains and soft pink paintwork provide a garden theme which reflects the sunshine's warmth and invites the outside in. Traditional bathroom furniture and fittings are essential ingredients in the Victorian country revival, so popular at present. The claw-foot, free-standing bath tub, standing in isolated splendour, is positioned centre-stage to provide the focal point. Taps and fittings should be in keeping (either brass or chrome) with white porcelain fitments. There are good reproductions and these are widely available. Shower attachments can be added to make decorative (yet functional) pipework a detail of period charm. The hand basin can be either generously proportioned pedestal-style or built into a suitable wooden surround or period vanity unit, with tiled splashback. The toilet seat should be of polished wood, and brass fittings should reflect on equipment, lighting, cupboards and door handles. Wooden flooring is practical in the bathroom and decorative rugs can become a feature. Wicker furniture is also steam resistant and correct for the period, and turns your bathroom into a private sitting-room.

Victorian fixtures look especially at home in a bathroom designed
in a traditional classical style. Pedestal sinks, with brass taps and
fixtures, fit naturally into this design scheme. Even new
reproductions can create the spirit of the old, when moulded and
encased in a mahogany surround to give a detailed finished look.
The visual impact can be softened, as here, with small petite fleur
bows on the wallpaper, and a rich glazed chintz floral print on the
curtain. The Victorian theme has been highlighted with an antique
lace blind, framed silhouette miniatures, country botanical prints,
plus silver picture mounts, books and ceramics for soaps or pot-
pourri. An antique bowl and pitcher makes an ideal accessory for a
stunning flower arrangement, adding colour and freshness to the
bathroom.

If your family is large, getting into the bathroom maybe a struggle, and once there maintaining pole position for any length of time can be equally problematical. Therefore, the planning of your bathroom, for not only space, colour and decoration, but for who will use it, and when, is important. If time and sharing are major problems, with perhaps different generations and sexes, then perhaps you should consider separate areas as a solution. Perhaps a shower and toilet can be installed downstairs, or *en suite* to avoid domestic discord. If additional space is a problem, but more than one person needs to use the bathroom at the same time, then two smaller sinks (as illustrated here) could be useful, with a large shared mirror and fitted cupboard or shelves on either side to provide a home for clutter. Pretty details can still add those special 'Country Style' features: a collection of Staffordshire dogs; ferns and plants; rich patterned lattice wallcovering. The room should feel cosy and reflect a feeling of privacy – even locked away from the rest of the house. A view of the garden can improve the whole awakening and bathing experience. However, privacy is essential: here a fringed festoon blind is both practical and decorative.

Left
The grandness of the large open
fireplace is reflected in the furnishings:
Victorian 'Art and Crafts' print has
been used to cover the chairs and
cushions; brass lamps; photo frames;
collectable clutter, from all parts of the
globe; oriental plates; jade figures and
brass and bronze curios – all reflect the
interests of a well-travelled occupant.
The blue and white meat dishes are
used decoratively, to add a delicate
touch to rough wall surfaces of brick
and stone.

Below
Whether restoring features that exist in
your house, or adding back period
details that create the correct mood and
style, panelling in oak or pine is a
wonderful reflection of Country Style.
It conveys a caring permanence that
few other features can achieve with
success. Panelling in England dates
back to the twelfth and thirteenth
centuries. Many of our stately homes
and castles were panelled and carved
with symbols of fertility or nature's
bounty of corn, fruits and vines, coats
of arms; initials or dates were other
common devices, used to mark out
moments in time or the passage of the
seasons. By Tudor times the fashion for
panelling had spread, as timber was
widely available. Oak panelling was
used for screens, to line walls and as
internal partitions to make large rooms
smaller. The panels would usually be
set into a timber sill at the base, and a
frieze or moulded beam at the top,
creating an effect which developed into
what is now known as a linen fold. The
sixteenth century saw the development
of linen fold (or 'wavy woodwork' as it
was called) into a fine art. These effects
were reproduced in Victorian times,
and although panelling can be
produced in different periods, different
vintages work together as harmonious
elements, creating a rich backdrop for
paintings, books and prints and
providing a finished surface that needs
little attention, if perhaps the
occasional waxing.

The stripped-down look focuses attention on stonework and window detail, to highlight a window or room with a view, to soften austerity with ample fabric swagged and draped. Pleated detail with both large and small rosette and airily arranged furniture and objects achieve a Gothic, almost monastic, serenity in this country house interior. But these principles can be developed and applied in far less grand settings than illustrated. A large floral with striped-back print in three scales has been used. The large full print for curtains, pleated and draped to full effect will impart a feeling of richness. The medium scale co-ordinate is ideal for cushions or upholstery, with refined tailoring detail, to fit furniture upholstery or, as here, window cushions, with a decorative pleating treatment as an attached decorative valance. The smallest scale is picked up as wall-coverings which gives a feeling of surface interest, yet acts as a colour carrier to allow prints or pictures, mirrors or lighting to detail the room without distraction. Architecture can be allowed to remain the main focus but it is on the details that the eye must linger. The carved chair back, antique globe, a chess board with the game unfinished, and an open book (left folded at a page), a Gothic mirror, and a marvellous flower arrangement: each object conveys its own individual story.

Above and opposite

Flowery chintz curtains, embroidered table-cloths, an oriental carpet, screen or prints, oil paintings, classical sculptures or guilt-edged mirrors, soft 'all over' upholstered chairs with tasselled cushions on these features unmistakably establish a classical country mood. While a cornice moulding to ceilings, high skirting boards painted white, a marble fireplace adding timeless grandeur, an antique display case, period furniture and fine porcelain all convey English style of the eighteenth century. The classical 'Age of Elegance'. The accent was on comfort, even cosiness. There was a similar emphasis on unity of colour and form. The English architect Robert Adam left some remarkable buildings, but also an imposing number of carefully conceived designs for interiors, with their myriad details. His ceilings, doorways, fireplaces, columns and carpets all reveal a lively and inventive use of strong colour. Adam's coloured ceilings represented the height of fashion. He juxtaposed brilliant colours with more subdued tones and applied them to walls and carpets to create a balanced whole. As an alternative to paint, paper could be used on walls for insulation as well as decoration. A typical mid-eighteenth century example would have probably been produced by Woodblock. Its immediate ancestors being the Chinese papers which twinkled with trees, blossoms and birds, like the painted silk hangings which inspired them. A combination of strong colour, yellow with a simple stencil of swags and bows, together with a white moulded cornice to frame the ceiling, blue-toned curtains and carpets, provides a clean contrast for the bright colours in the embroidery, table-cloth, pottery and prints.

Opposite above and above

These two illustrations convey a similar mood yet achieve it in completely different ways. One is highly frilled and fancy, printed co-ordinated fabric is used on the table top, window curtains, frills, cushions and upholstery, combined with a patterned carpet, rugs and striped simple wall-covering. But note how the yellow has been used as a plain colour to create unity: plainly used on sofa, screen and table lampshades, carrying the colour to all parts of the room. Chairs and tables as well as decorative objects are placed to create mirror image on either side of the featured oil painting; thus allowing other walls to reflect collective clutter and where activity is taking place, rather than relaxation.

Compare this to the simplicity of style, where plain white walls allow for the sculptural shapes of the windows to form their own decorative effect, and a light openness has been created in the airiness of the room. Simple symmetry has been used in the same way to create an orderly sense of luxury – selectivity is the secret to integrating furnishing of any style, and colour schemes can either pull the entire room together or create an interesting diversity depending on the mood you wish to create and your personal tastes.

Opposite below

The country hearth or fireplace is the focus of a room, a promise of toasty warmth and comfort; few can resist its welcoming glow on cold winter evenings – whether you long for the wonderful crackle and aroma of burning logs or the satisfying embers of a coal fire. Few will shun their inviting presence of homeliness. There is something magical about a fireplace, it becomes a gathering point for the family, a fire invites you into the central position in a room – once there you can turn your back on it, and feel you have arrived and are at home. Nothing else can lure you more, and nothing can mesmerize you more by the unique 'magic lantern' effect of dancing flames, in seeming perpetual motion, as its unique colours dance, make shadows and shapes to beguile and fascinate those who willingly succumb to the proud presence of the mantelpiece or open grate.

Above left
Who could resist sitting down to dinner at this table? Certainly not anyone who loves traditional styling. A simple rectangular table has been bedecked with fine crystal glass, which glitters like a mirror in candlelight, making dining a romantic intimate occasion. Co-ordinated designs used on upholstery, curtains and wall-covering give the room unity of colour and style, setting a tone of opulence so dear to the hearts of the traditionalist with high values who possesses the essential attention to detail.

Above right
Simple country ladder-backed chairs and a table setting on an antique lace tablecloth. A small ceramic bowl brimming with lovely flowers, fine wine, cut glass, and the candles ready to light. Simple pretty poppy motif curtains have been used as the inspiration for stencil work to highlight a secluded corner with interest. The late autumn sunlight adds the final ingredient to the evening's dining pleasure.

Opposite
Dining-rooms that have the considerable advantage of simple wood panelling create a mood of historical splendour. Panelling with sunk-framed squares or rectangles were popular in the sixteenth and seventeenth century, and is still made today using seventeenth-century methods. It can transform a modest dining area into a real country house atmosphere. With oak table and chairs, silver candlesticks, cut glass and oil paintings the room reflects heritage, and dining here can be sheer delight.

Left, above and below
The need to create a special place in most homes reflects not only the busy life we lead at work, which has a tendency to spill over into our home life, but also the need domestically to utilize rooms for multi-purpose activities. Therefore, in a growing number of homes an at-home office, a quiet study in which to relax, a sewing room or studio in which to work can be created. A room for reading or reflective study or for personal escape. In designing a personal space, you will want to consider your needs carefully. You will need space to work, a desk, chair, and a place to relax, with easy chairs, *chaise-longue* or sofa bed – with the ability to turn your room into a guest room if required. Storage should also be considered, a desk can disguise personal items, but you may need fitted book shelves, for reference books or photographs, or side cupboards to accommodate larger items. A relaxed atmosphere can be created with curtains, upholstery and cushions in functional stripes or floral print chintz, woven fabrics and needlepoint cushions. Drama can be created with a reefed curtain effect on a window pole, this also has the added advantage of allowing more light into your room. Rugs can also make a decorative statement whether 'oriental' or 'Kelim'. A simple plain carpet gives added comfort and luxury to your room. Lighting is another important factor, and will largely be dependent on your overall design scheme. Rooms decorated either traditionally or with country clutter, easily accommodate desk lamps, table or wall-hung lamps, with shades of frosted glass, fabric, moiré silk or paper. These still look appropriate in more modern homes, but designers might prefer a more monocromatic shade that matches the colour of the walls. Bright white or clean colours are ideal for workrooms, as they stimulate thought and allow for richness to come from fabrics, carpets and personal clutter. An impersonal yet workmanlike room may not have many accessories, where as a more relaxed environment may have many. Whatever you decide will be highly personal but may include family photographs, portrait oil paintings or landscapes, ceramic or wooden sculptures, Victorian oil lamps, a small clock, barometer, or perhaps a musical instrument – all make ideal decorative objects.

Against a painted background of misty green an assortment of patterns creates a comfortable environment that reflects Country Style at its best. Richness and clutter selected with flair and fashionable skill have blended to create a room full of interest, yet which is as personal as a finger print. The plainness of the walls, woodwork and sheets allow the rich patterns to be the dominant feature. Rich, printed fabrics, patchwork bedspread and heavy, deep-patterned carpeting enlivens this bedroom, adding grandeur and scale to create atmosphere and style, which reinforces the casual rustic mood of the room. The twin lamps and twin chairs give the room stability and order by planking a regiment of old prints, set out like soldiers on parade, all is orderly and rather formal in contrast to the country casualness of the room's furnishings. Accessories can be a key element adding personal touches to your home. In this setting the breakfast tray seems most natural and inviting for a friendly morning conversation over tea and toast, with the morning letters or perhaps the Sunday papers.

Simple bedwear design in Country Diary Poppy (by Dorma) on bedlinen, co-ordinating curtains and matching small-print wallpaper complement the collectable clutter, on the side tables, walls and overmantel. The whole mood is Victorian. Most of the furniture can be obtained easily from antique or specialist decor shops. Items such as the cast-iron bed, fire surround and fender, together with the painted pine table, are available to those who know where to look. Pine upright chair, armchair and towel rail, all originated in the Victorian era. In this cosy bedroom corner personal clutter is all important to create the Victorian mood. For example, silver scent bottles, candlesticks, hair brush and comb set, jug and bowl, cushions, linens, pictures, prints and even your favourite doll, all have their place here. Country comfort is completed by the presence of the open fire, giving warmth to autumn evenings, and the casual scattering of rugs on pine-planked flooring, and flowers both dried and natural. The subdued lighting completes this picture of a Victorian country cottage bedroom at its best. One must remember that having the warmth and friendliness of an open fire in your bedroom, and the comfort which this brings, turns your bedroom into a place for reading, writing letters, or relaxing, thus creating a multi-purpose room rather than just a place to sleep.

Country manor conveys a spirit of Englishness that we all strive to
retain and recreate in our special interior rooms. It is the traditions
and wealth of fine objects, furniture, paintings, tapestries, coverlets
and silk, brocaded woven carpets in faded rich colours, fabrics
festooned at large, light, well-proportioned windows or expensively
on table tops to convey an atmosphere of rich heritage and
grandeur. The high-backed sculptural brass bed takes centre stage in
this setting, fitted with ruffled bed dressings of satin or silk and
chintz fabrics, creating a feeling of the English manor house in the
late eighteenth century. If you wished to create this room be
generous with traditional fabrics and rich colours as your aim is to
create a feeling of opulence and indulgence.

With the development of high-quality mattresses and the divan base the decorative bed and bedroom has returned with the growth of the duvet (a Continental sleeping habit) that took hold with the rise of polyester/ cotton easycare fabric in the late sixties. Today's bedrooms have developed into a unique experience, and everyone's room displays a personal character of its own. Whether your choice is a four-poster bed in brass, or a decorative wooden bed as shown here, the variety of styles are as endless as the variety of linen to dress it. Manufacturers produce a wide range of quality plain and printed co-ordinates in bedlinen, curtains and tableware, bedspreads, towels and bathrobes, in beautiful fibres such as silks, cotton and linens. Design ranges from traditional concepts such as 'The Country Diary Collection' produced by Dorma, to the creamy elegance of crafted lace, and exclusive ranges of cottons and silks from high-fashion designer names.

Wallpaper and fabric elements of the Country Diary 'Autumntide' design are combined to form a restful and harmonious surround for a collection of period country objects, including a hand-painted rocker, an old hat-box used as a bedside table and Victorian pressed-flower pictures.

STENCILLING

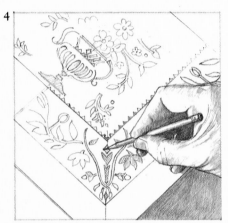

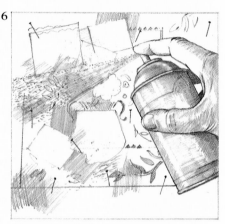

1 Drawing up your design
Having selected your subject, sketch out the design. Think of flat simple shapes, do not get too complex, since the flattening of the image makes a shape easier to copy and cut. Make a tracing if you wish.

2 Blocking in and bridging
Having drawn up your idea, you must clarify the areas you need to cut away. This is best achieved by 'blocking in', shading or cross hatching to make distinction easier. These areas once blocked in will present your final design. Intact linking pieces or 'bridges' are essential to give the stencil strength and stability. You can now transfer your design on to a piece of stencil card – manila card soaked in linseed oil makes the best stencils.

3 Cutting the stencil
You now need to cut away your blocked-in shapes, and for this you will need a good craft knife or scalpel. Begin in the centre of the design. Cut smaller shapes first and keep the hand behind the blade for safety and always cut towards you. Work with a smooth action and take your time. If you make a cutting slip, masking tape can be used on both sides to rejoin the stencil. Use 'self healing' cutting board for this part of the operation.

4 Borders and corners
When stencilling a border, you will need to design a corner piece to link horizontal and vertical stretches. These will have to be measured to fit with existing borders. Construct a new stencil from a square piece of card, draw the two right angles, an inner and an outer, that form a 'frame' exactly the width of the border pattern. Leaving the corner blank, place your cut border stencil within the frame on either side of the corner, and draw or spray enough of the pattern to design a central motif that will link the border on both sides. To repeat or join a border, draw a length of border design on stencil card leaving several inches of blank card at either end. Cut out the design and bend the card round to form a loop, and slide one end under the other until they locate. Using the holes in the outer layer as a guide, draw in the linking shapes, then unwind the card and cut them out.

5 Attaching the stencil

Once your stencil is complete ensure that all edges of the design are flush to the surface on which you wish to stencil before you start to spray or apply the paint. This stops the paint seeping under the edges and blurring your clean outline. An aerosol adhesive or spray mount can be applied to the reverse side, and this in turn applied to the surface to be stencilled. This makes the stencil tacky but not permanently glued, thus several stencils can be made before re-spraying. Dressmaker's pins can be used to attach the stencil. Once in place seal the edges with masking tape to make firm contact. Then protect the surrounding surfaces around the stencil with lining paper or newspaper. Check all surfaces are protected ready for spraying.

6 Spraying your stencil

Remember a little goes a long way. With the spray nozzle 3in-6in (7.5cm-15cm) from the stencil, a light gentle pumping movement on the nozzle button will produce a light spray. Avoid large blotches or runny paint. It is best to use thin layers of paint and build up the colour slowly. You can spray your motif in just one colour, or use many colours and build up a more complex three-dimensional effect with several shades and colours, masking out areas from time to time with newsprint. Paint can also be applied by stippling, or dabbed lightly with a sponge, but spray paint is the most effective method, as it is quick drying and durable. There is no need to clean a stencil after use, simply remove it and let it dry.

Above

The finished stencil can be used time and time again to decorate cushions or fabrics, shelves, table-tops or furniture generally or applied to walls; either covered with a plain lining paper or directly on to the plaster – if the surface is sound. Stencils can be used as a frieze on walls or floors, or on a free-standing screen for dividing areas of a room; for privacy or simply to create a decorative feature.

Decorative use of the stencil technique for trays, pictures, frames, stationery or lampshades can add that personal touch to your room decor.

Left
Here a small stencil tile effect has been used to create an elusion of a dado rail. and a pretty country rose border has been stencilled as a ceiling cornice to frame Victorian prints. Tassel cords and ribbon and bows have been applied to add a decorative feature. This delicate detailing can be highly personal and yet most effective in its simplicity.

Below
Pine furniture can sometimes appear large and imposing in a small kitchen. Its usefulness can sometimes be questioned. But with a little time and effort, stencilling can make its size seem smaller and the decorative effect can be most pleasing, adding charm, using traditional motifs of fruit and flowers, to add rustic authenticity to country furniture.

CREATIVE CUSHIONS

A cushion not only adds comfort and softness to otherwise hard pieces of furniture, but can also be used as an important part in the decoration of a room. Cushions can be used dramatically to add a splash of colour to a nursery or plain monochromatic room scheme, or to add clutter to a traditional chintz sitting-room, picking up co-ordinating fabrics or colours to convey richness to interiors by creating comfort and charm. Cushions can be changed easily, and are considered a secondary accent, therefore you can use them to reflect the colours of the changing seasons to offset the mood by using warm, rich colours in winter, and cool sharp pastels in summer. Cushions can also create mood and atmosphere in a room. Pretty lace can be attached to convey feminine softness and gentle romance when scattered on a bed with traditional satin sheets and fluffy pillows. However, a firm box-cushion upholstery in a ticking stripe creates a more masculine smartness for studio or deck. Historic moods can be created with tassel detail attached to corners in a Victorian setting, or classical format. Kelim weave in rich varied earth tones, piped or corded can create a more ethnic feel to blend with oak or antique furnishing. Large floor cushions can be used for extra seating if space is a problem.

Illustrated here are a few examples of cushion edgings to suit your personal decorative ideas and interiors.

1 Cord-edged cushion.
2 Frilled with bias binding edging.
3 Piped cushion with tassel corners.
4 Satin Oxford edge with lace inset and appliqué embroidery.
5 Scalloped-edged cushion with ribbon binding and top-stitched detail.
6 Velvet box cushion with pleated edges and buttoned.
7 Corded cushion with tailored pinch-pleated frill.
8 Circular lace-edged cushion, ribbon-quilted with bows.

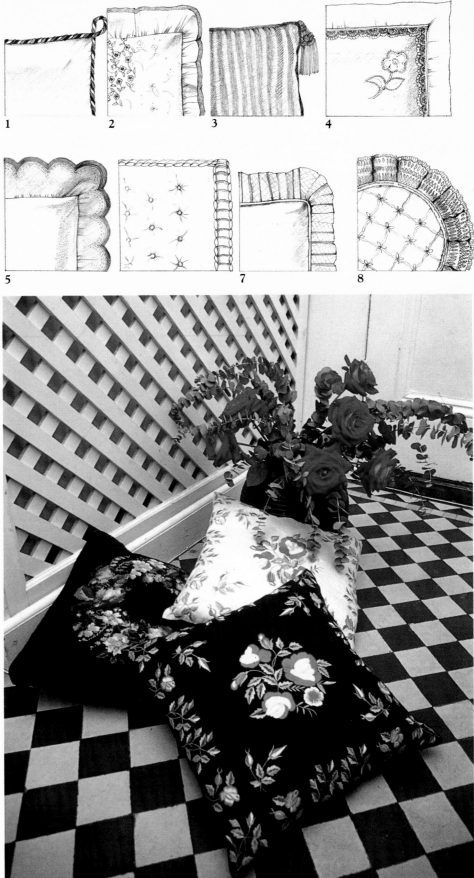

FURNITURE AND UPHOLSTERY

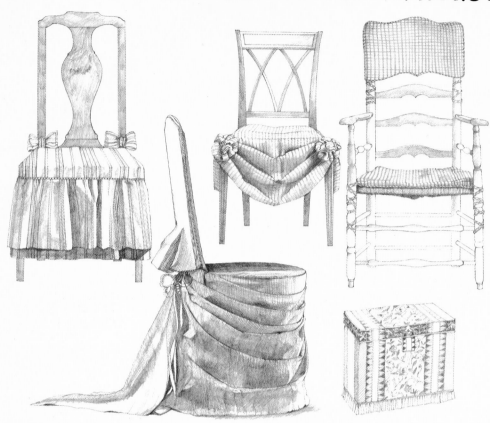

Comfortable seating is essential, but it has to be designed to suit our various activities, whether we are dining, working, or relaxing. The seating you choose will reflect your mood, and suit your purpose. Supporting your body is a chair or sofa's main function, but the designer's inventiveness seems to hold no bounds. However ingenious the designer may contort the look and style of a chair – comfortable it must be.

Hemlines (frills and fabric)
Above
Dressing up chairs in party-frock frills and fancy bows, pencil pleats, swagged, bustled and ribboned is a useful decorative tip. Chairs can be dressed up to co-ordinate with a room's colours and fabrics, adding comfort and style to your interior decor. An ottoman can also be a useful storage trunk, lined and upholstered. It also can be used for additional seating in a small room.

Bed-sits
Below
Comfortable, padded tub chairs or bedroom chairs, short legged and frilled, in plain and fancy fabrics are most suitable in bed-sits. They are shaped for comfort and decorated in style, button-backed or neatly trimmed. These chairs are ideal for occasional sitting in the bedroom, dressing-room or bed-sitting room.

Cushioned comfort (suites, sofas for the living-room)
Left
There are many comfortable settees, sofas and three-piece suites on the market today, far more than can be illustrated here, but the essential ingredients for any comfortable easy chair are cushions. The two sofas here are scroll armed with collectable cushions in a sweeping serpentine curve; the scroll arms are typical of the early nineteenth century. Well-designed prints are numerous; meticulous tailoring and a superior construction give elegance, grace and lasting comfort.

Antique and tasselled (for that period look)
Below
A Queen Anne wing chair is a fine example of the many period styles that are classically antique. In general, embellishments have not been spared to create a sumptuous piece of furniture or upholstery. The 'antique and tasselled' freely blends the use of rich fabrics with detailed carved mouldings and rich accessories of fringes, buttons and cording.

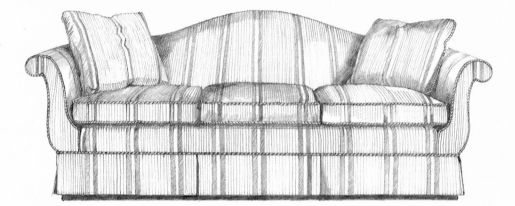

Christmas

WINTER

WINTER

Like as the thrush in winter, when the skies
Are drear and dark, and all the woods are bare,
Sings undismayed, till from his melodies
Odours of spring float through the frozen air;—
So in my heart when sorrow's icy breath
Is bleak and bitter and its frost is strong,
Leaps up, defiant of despair and death
A sunlit fountain of triumphant song.
Sing on sweet singer till the violets come
And south winds blow, sing on prophetic bird!
O if my lips, which are for ever dumb
Could sing to men what my sad heart has heard
Life's darkest hour with songs of joy would ring,
Life's blackest frost would blossom into Spring
Edmond Holmes

Winter means days cold and bright, frosty mornings, misty light, tints of grey and white, snow-covered roofs. Falling leaves of rich brown hues, auburn tinted; red-breasted robins and blue tits pecking at bottle tops and bird tables; hazel nuts and acorns stored by scampering squirrels for winter food till spring returns. The winter warmth of holly berries, bright red against deep green. Decorations in halls and stairs and reception rooms welcoming the traditions of Christmas and the season of goodwill. Trees bare of leaf facing the frozen air are in stark contrast to the log fire that cheers and warms our hearth and home.

Opposite and below
Natural surfaces have been left exposed to capture that country cottage style, by retaining much of the character and charm of the original building's shape and structure. The warm tones of plaster, paint and wood, are enhanced by carefully planned lighting, taking full advantage of both natural light and artificial additions, allowing the simple sturdiness of the hall and staircase to become a focus of unpretentious charm. These important spaces, therefore, acquire a dignity they richly deserve but seldom achieve. In winter's decorative colour scheme, textures and surfaces are all important; stone walls, plaster and oak timbers, create a feeling of timeless space, like a snow-covered landscape covered by a sharp frost with dark divisions of walls and hedges, silhouetted against the sky. The typical country cottage style is similar in feeling – lean, sparse and pared-down-to-basics, stripped oak panels, whitewashed walls. The colours are limited, yet the contrasting textures are all important. Furniture too has a functional place and a simplicity of style, comfortable yet practical. Natural colours can be added to enhance any room by bringing the outside inside with displays of winter foliage in vase or pitcher.

Above and below right
Winter interiors need not mean starkness and coldness. Colours can be incorporated to create a warm and inviting atmosphere. Think of the great variety of colours and shades in an Oriental rug which can add vitality and cosiness to your hallways and corridors.

Deep rich colours can be used on paintwork and walls to create a unique blend of grandeur and informality and provide a strong background for fine paintings, portraits or to highlight an ornamental staircase, ceiling cornice or light centre-piece.

HEARTH AND HOME

Here little has been altered from the cottage's original construction. Beams have been left exposed to create a background structure to interspace brickwork and plaster, forming a natural surface interest to this charming old fireplace. The huge wooden over-mantel is a sculptural presense in the room through its dominant feature – softened with country accents and clutter, Staffordshire dogs, Victorian clock, candlesticks, mugs and family photo's bedeck the mantel-shelf. An open log fire-grate completes the picture of a warm atmosphere that is inviting on winter evenings, to relax and gather round, as in days gone by; when life centred around the fireside hearth. Colourful fresh flowers and clusters of dried flowers bedeck beams and table-top. Twin comfortable armchairs covered in a country print, which co-ordinates with the window drapes, convey traditional country character.

Above

Today's fires and fireplaces can be really stylish. They can reflect traditional or contemporary tastes and suit every type of home, whether it is a country cottage or bed-sit, flat or Georgian mews. Nothing beats the immediate warmth and cosiness of a real fire on winter evenings. Many styles and uses are incorporated in today's fires from open hearth, which can add background, warmth and focus, to convection fires which also provide radiant heat. There are stoves and room heaters that burn wood and solid fuel, with real flames flickering behind closed glass door's. The pot-belly, cast-iron stove has grown increasingly popular over recent years, and is no longer the sole property of the starving artist in his attic garret. All over the country people are rediscovering the allure of wood-burning stoves in country kitchen or homely living-room. Whereas gas and oil mainly heat the air – wood radiates heat, and actually warms people. Realistic 'log-burning' gas fires have become very popular in smokeless zone areas, and where maintenance must be kept to a minimum.

Right

The country manor grandeur of open-hearth fires in every room can be created in just one sitting-room today, thanks to efficient central heating, which gave people the freedom of their homes, as warmth is developed from behind rather than from in front of a fire. Grand room proportions reflected in windows, doors and classic carved fireplace surrounds can be reduced in size by using strong deep wall colours, creating richness and opulence. Finishing touches include paintings, carpets and comfortable furniture, porcelain and personal memento's acquired from travels, or family heirlooms.

An early authentic workman's cottage; a small kitchen/dining room practical and completely functional, naturally simple and original in construction and character. The room's warm-toned colours are reflected in the rays of the fire. In the old days this single room was the centre of family life, the 'hub of the home'. Life centred around the fireplace and the kitchen, because it was both the source of not only warmth but also light and food. Seating was arranged around the fireplace, with either simple Windsor chairs, pine settee or bench. Practical flooring of pine and stone flags, scrubbed or wax finished reflects an aged patina of time, giving the room a genuine character. The furniture is of a simple construction, sturdy, robust and basic, reflecting the simple economy that existed in times past. This down-to-earth simplicity has a tremendous attraction when contrasted with today's rush-and-hassle environment.

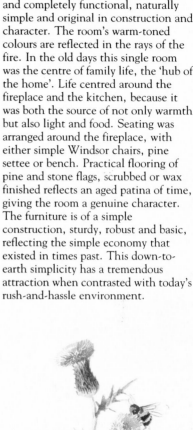

COUNTRY BARNS

Above, left and right
In contrast, many country barn
conversions offer the decorative
opportunity to expand the country-
style kitchen from its once small
intimacy to a grand scale with every
conceivable unit built-in to create the
living/kitchen room, though retaining
practicality and convenience with
impressive structural features of height
and spaciousness. A far cry from the
thrift and economy of early country
folk.

The solid fuel stove seems somehow to symbolize the epitome of cottage life. It warms the room, dries herbs and autumn flowers, clothes and towels. It can cook all things from baked potatoes to the Christmas turkey, puddings and country stews. It keeps everything warm and dry and also heats the water for washing up, or bathing (a far cry from the cast-iron range, kettle hob and the tin bath brought in from the coal shed). This practical piece of kitchen equipment seems to bring life and pleasure to today's country kitchen, creating a homely corner of homespun charm.

Above and right

Country-style bathrooms can sometimes be located in a converted bedroom, though purpose-built bathrooms can also be an extension on the ground floor; usually they are spacious and comfortable, which invites you to linger longer over your bathing. Larger bathrooms can contain a side stool for seating to allow time to relax in lazy comfort. Practical tiling on floor and walls is essential where water is in abundance as moisture and steam can cause problems if wood surfaces are not adequately varnished or protected. Simple tile patterns are most practical in small areas behind baths, toilets or hand basins and small tiles fit well into small nooks and crannies. Choose muted colours for your bathroom. Soft pinks, green or sea blue, or white for that clean sparkle. Remember house plants thrive in a steamy atmosphere, and therefore the bathroom is an ideal medium. Rather surprisingly it provides an excellent gallery for displays of your favourite ceramic plates, figures or pottery, mugs and bowls. All of which will not be effected by moisture. Also collections of pebbles, shells, bottles or soaps create plenty of interest to amuse while soaking in the tub. The centre of this stage is however the bath itself. Deep sided and generous, either free standing in the centre of the room or to one side. Gleaming white enamel with traditional fittings in gold or chrome, at the side of which you can feature a traditional bathroom rug or exotic carpet to create an accent of colour and spice. Alternatively, the understated sophistication of Scandinavian pine, co-ordinating hand basin and stark decoration is very effective.

NAUTICAL COUNTRY

Above

A crisp winter's morning and the soft rays of subdued sunlight shine through an open window, creating a fresh new morning atmosphere, and brighten a cool corner. Thick stonework whitewashed walls are spick and span, typical of English nautical country charm. Wood can be painted if built into the room. Here a charming book case alcove has been colourfully washed out in sea blue and detailed in white paint. Natural pine sailor's chests are ideal for additional storage and make useful tables, and even seats. It is important to retain a closeness to nature in 'nautical' homes. The sensuality of the landscape and surroundings outside invade the cool interiors. The clarity of lightness inspires a feeling of spacious charm.

Opposite and right

Nautical country reflects a house or home belonging to someone who lives and works by the sea or by one of our many inland waterways, Fenland broads or River Weir. The uninhibited use of colours is a major factor in nautical country (due to frequent contact with water), rich faded tones of arms and heraldic pennants, flags of chivalry and pageantry. Figurative carvings in oak and pine, or constructions of boats and models. A love of gadgets and purposeful materials woven or crafted in practical objects like ropes, netting or sailcloth. Everything hand-made from wood casks to metal weather vanes. Like a ship's chandlers, the nautical country cottage contains a storehouse of necessities, a fitness of purpose to support a simple life-style. Evidence of the nearness to water or the seashore will be obvious inside a nautical home. Collections of fishing floats, netting, pebbles or shells may be on display. Baskets for storage of logs and odds and ends. Painted furniture – chests of drawers or chair backs, stencils (boats and flags) used on kitchen cupboards and walls.

Traditional harmony in the country house drawing-room has been
achieved with *objects d'art* creating small cameo displays against a
background of wood panelling interspersed with a traditional woven
tapestry screen and Kelim cushions. Watercolour pictures cover
every bit of wall space and the objects tend to be beautiful and
valuable rather than bric-a-brac. The vase of flowers also helps to
make this a comfortable corner in which to relax.

Traditional winter colour schemes and furnishing fabrics have been combined with patchwork cushions and needlepoint to create a comfortable and very distinctive ambience. Strong green has been applied with a rag-rolled effect to provide a contrast to white paintwork. Framed botanical prints therefore become more visible by the contrast of light and dark; concealed lighting has been used behind the oak overmantel to create a fireplace feature.
Comfortable chairs surround the warm, friendly log fire, creating the perfect mood for entertaining friends or relations, for sharing thoughts and good conversation.

IN THE GRAND MANOR

Above

The winter drawing-room is the traditional, comfortable gathering room for the family at Christmas. An open fire is an ideal element to create a relaxed and warm atmosphere, providing not only essential warmth to combat winter's chill, but is a vital focal point in the room, for gathering together family and friends for that magic moment of opening presents on Christmas morning, for after-dinner drinks or afternoon tea and muffins. This relaxing gracious room is essential to family life. A simple arrangement of comfortable chairs and tables is all that is required together with traditional country prints to give colour and harmony. Deep colours create a mood of relaxed luxury and reflect traditional values of heritage and taste. Here is English Country Style illustrated at its most comfortable and gracious. Pretty floral chintz covers the

chesterfield, wing chairs and side stools. There are co-ordinating table-cloths in both matching printed and plain fabrics; the latter being used for cushions as well. The rich magenta has been used to contrast with black lacquer panelling, and to highlight delicate ceiling cornices and decorative plaster work. Lighting is achieved by wall lights, central chandelier and side lamps, giving different levels for different activities.

Opposite

Country Diary Country Garden fabrics and wallpapers warm this room. Rich plum colours in the dried flowers, the picture and the rug give an effective focus in an otherwise subtle colour scheme.

141

Above and left

The quaint and curious have always been the corner-stone of English life, with country craftsmen producing objects for practical use or just plain decoration. Today there is a major revival in many of these crafts and a renewed market for traditional objects. This has been mainly due to the revival and renewed interest in colonial American folk art which was born out of a pioneering spirit, of practicality and inventiveness, with limited materials and simple tools. This ornamental look embraces function and uncluttered simplicity, using paint and wood, plaster and metal to create pattern and objects more akin to folk art traditions than refined sophisticated cultures. Typical are simple country subjects, animals, fruit and flowers and landscapes which can be applied to wooden cut-outs. Furniture can be stencilled or painted. Gilding and glazing create the period mood. Flat colours can be ragged or dragged, and surfaces stippled or crazed to give a distressed old quality to objects that makes them barely distinguishable from their originals. The most suitable collectable pieces tend to be chosen for their rarity value, or detail quality, and these reproductions are of a high standard of finish. Bronze urns, planters, lamps, carved woodwork, ornate mirrors – all can be expertly produced. Today, over a century after the industrial revolution made the artisan obsolete, we are witnessing a rebirth of traditional craft and hand-made objects, which represent a 'back-to-basics' movement which urges a way of life that recaptures the simplicity of the past and, like collectables, country curios can enrich your decorative options.

CHRISTMAS FARE

Table decorations are particularly colourful and last a considerable time, with the added advantage that after dining they still look attractive on a shelf or window-sill. Simple bowls of holly, with dried leaves or silk flowers, pine cones or tree bark, can be used to create a Christmas display of traditional colours. Candlesticks can also be decorated (using mastic) to anchor sprays and garlands into position. But be careful, for dried flowers can be very inflammable, so use tall candles and artifical berries, beads and tinsel. The colours of winter and Christmas time are red and green: red ribbon, candles and berries, green leaves of holly, laurel and fir Christmas trees. Their inherent richness conveys the comfort of traditional values.

Above

Lighting can give atmosphere, creating the correct mood for the occasion. It will vary depending on the activities the room accommodates. In dining areas lighting can generally be lower, but nothing can evoke the mood of Christmas more than the light of candles, which create a close intimacy and bring traditional values to that most traditional of family occasions. Who could resist sitting down to Christmas dinner at this table? Certainly good food and wine are in evidence, but anyone who loves traditional styling will approve of this scene: a decorative festive table-cloth, sweetmeats and holly berries reflecting the candlelight, bathing the scene with the shadows of the season, warming the room and creating a cosiness that befits the occasion. The family is reminded at dinner of past good times, bringing, symbolically at least, the spirit of Christmas to this festive meal with friends and family.

Right

However Christmas is celebrated, few people can resist the special spirit which belongs to this time of year. There is scarcely a home where people do not make some effort to cheer themselves with Christmas decor and decorations. The approach is naturally very personal, and the extent of Christmas indulgence knows no bounds. However, some will make do with a simple tree, or a branch of holly or mistletoe here and there, while others will festoon the whole house with ribbons and streamers. Fruit can be most decorative on a Christmas dining-table, adding natural colours and country fare. Enhancing walls and table-top, doors and fireplace overmantel all add traditional character with an understated informality; silver candlesticks and plate sparkle in the candlelight or in winter sunlight, creating an intimate atmosphere for this festive dining occasion.

Opposite
Crisp blue and white fabrics and ceramics create a cool feeling of
freshness. Crinkly bed dressings are soft and inviting, pretty
scalloped pillowcases and a beautiful quilted bedspread reflect
simplicity of style. Careful grouping of patterns creates a romantic
harmony with winter white nets at the window to give maximum
light to a small bedroom. The sculptural cast-iron bed head with
brass embellishments is the centre of attention in this Country Style
bedroom.

Above
Here stripes and flowers have been skilfully used by the designer, to
give harmony of colour and style. The blue and white stripe is used
to carry colour to all surfaces in the room, from bed covering,
window blinds and wallpaper to the lamp shade. White paintwork
is the natural choice. The large 'peony' flowers have been adapted
to all-over curtains (for a rich fullness). Wallpaper borders are at
ceiling cornice and dado height (to frame the room), and as a trellis
on the bed covering (to give a multi-layered effect).

Opposite
The bedroom corner evokes a feeling of quiet intimacy and, like a
still-life painting, the dressing-table reveals the delicate beauty of
Victorian lace. The opulence and the traditional nature of this
bedroom is enhanced by a profusion of pillows and bed covers,
embellished with wide ruffles. The lace fabric has been draped
gauze-like as a canopy. This skilful touch visually softens the room
and adds to its feeling of delicate charm.

Above
Warm sunlight filters through long lace curtains lighting up a room
of simple elegance – generous window treatments of frilled scalloped
pelmet, festoon blind and long tied back drapes, co-ordinated with
the printed duvet in another Country Diary design by Dorma. Frills
edge the pillows and cushions.

The wallpaper frieze has been used to create a 'dado' rail effect to
divide up the wall surfaces. The heavy printed effect is mellowed by
plain green painted walls, giving pictures a highlight or accent
effect when collected or clustered together.

Collectable country clutter created with a wealth of fine objects,
some personal and decorative, while others are practical in nature.

Attention to detail is important, and stamps your personality on
a room. Nimble fingers are in evidence here, whether by padding
the cast-iron headboard with a centre cameo of fabric, or arranging
fresh cut flowers to add natural colour and country freshness and
fragrance to your bedroom.

Cottage bedrooms like this create a haven from the work day toil,
creating a dreamworld of flowers and frills, mixing modern comforts
with traditional styling.

WINTER WHITES

Opposite and right
The all-white interior grew out of the twenties' vogue for monochromatic rooms. Its charm lay in the impression of lightness, and the sense of space that was created. But white rooms have a considerable disadvantage as they tend to need more maintenance to retain that all important freshness. Yet the white room is returning to popularity, due to easy-care fabrics and, for some, domestic help. The juxtaposition of fabrics – sculptured or woven, laced-edged or embroidered – gives the romantic feeling of pampered indulgence and delicacy. The light from either window or lamp enhances the figured materials to create a richness difficult to achieve with coloured or heavier patterned fabrics. The sculptural effect of furniture becomes more dramatically obvious in a room furnished in white fabrics, for little can detract or offend the eye. Decorative confidence can be achieved as the stunning effect created can show great care, personal pride and a delicate attention to detail.

Right
Nothing can quite compare with the smell of freshly laundered white linen. Crisp, clinically clean sheets and pillowcases bring country charm to any bedroom. Storage is also an important consideration. For, with a little thought, this too can make a positive contribution to the decor. Avoid the harsh, anonymous linen cupboard, a sturdy pine chest, particularly if colour-washed, is a delightful addition to any room. The storage of beautiful linen need not be something to confine to a spare bedroom – make it part of the overall design scheme of your room.

SURFACE TEXTURE

Country style is simple, and country living is experiencing old-fashioned delights. Homes were built of natural materials: wood, clay, brick, slate, thatch, plaster, stone and flint. All were constructed and used with a personal character which reflected an area of the country and its locality. All showed the mark of true craftsmanship and were in harmony with nature. These time-honoured reminders of our rich heritage are visually apparent all around us. Sadly, however, distinctive regional characteristics are being eroded as more and more houses are being built of brick and planning regulations become undisciplined and lax. When restoring your home and refurnishing it, seek out the original timbers, slates and brickwork wherever possible. Building yards and demolition reclaimers are the best source of materials. Think carefully before changing for changes sake only. Always put back rather than take away, but if 'progress' is required, then learn to live with natural materials as your first choice, for there is no substitute for the original. A home owner interested in preserving country style pays attention to detail. By making decorative use of things employed in the daily life of the past, any home can become a country retreat. 'The face of a house is the face of the man it was built for'. It shows his character, tastes, interest, wealth, fears and aspirations more clearly than anything he may say about himself. The house will reflect craftsmanship, materials, climate and a face of history, to change it, will alter evidence of the past. We do not, however, want to live in a museum, but in changing the face of history we must have a caring nature and an understanding of our traditional heritage. All that is needed is an affectionate respect for the ideas and workmanship of the original home.

CREATIVE LIGHTING

The quality of light affects our surroundings, therefore lighting effects around the house should be varied to suit working, relaxing or entertaining. Lighting represents the important third decorative dimension, after colour and design. Lighting can add mood, create atmosphere and transform space with the flick of a switch. Planning your lighting position is therefore a vital factor to consider in your decorative scheme. A versatile lighting plan is particularly important in a sitting-room, to accommodate use change. Remember down-lighters and pendant light give good general lighting, while indirect lighting from up-lighters can create atmosphere, whereas a spotlight, trackline or picture light will give specific emphasis to features around the room. Up-lights bounce a beam on to the ceiling for a soft, indirect light, whereas standard lamps and wall lights will cast a downward light to illuminate a specific area. Track-mounted spotlights create a flexible light source, which can be varied by moving them along the track where necessary. Clip-on spotlights can be used for working areas or to highlight features. Remember to avoid shadows cast by spotlights in kitchens and stairways, where the change from area of shadow to glare may be unsafe unless there is a general light source to give total illumination. Task lighting for writing, reading or sewing should be positioned so that light is reflected on to the work surface for comfortable indirect light. Remember that pendant lights, hung low over occasional tables or even dining tables, can create work-station lighting and substitute for table lamps thus leaving the surface clear for working. Artificial lighting has advanced considerably in design terms, far more than any other interior design element. The ingenuity of shape, design and application has developed into an art form, indeed some lighting can be classed as 'functional sculpture' (left). Lighting can be both attractive to look at and be made to alter shape and colour, it can distort or enhance, add drama or minimize fuss, increase working efficiently or create subtlety in mood and atmosphere.

General lighting

Gives overall shadowless light. You will need this type of lighting in rooms where there is a high level of activity, such as kitchens and family rooms, and in halls and stairways where safety is vitally important. They may not evoke a romantic mood, but they are essential for practical safety, and can obviously be supplemented by down-lighters or wall lights to transform a room at will. Simple ceiling-mounted glass globes or fluorescent tubes will provide sufficient light in small rooms, such as kitchens, bathrooms and utility rooms.

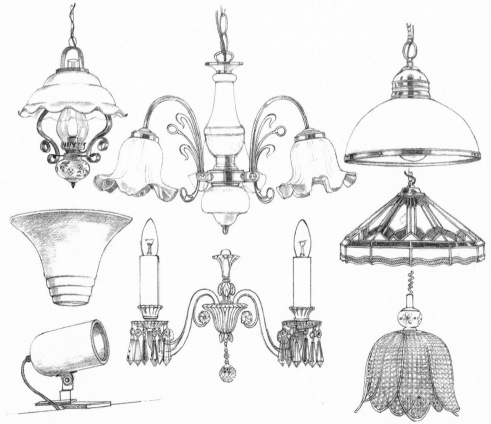

Task lighting
Gives specific light in work areas.
Spotlights can be used in conjunction
with general background lighting to
give prominence to a kitchen work
surface, work bench or desk. Strip
lights can be positioned each side of a
bathroom mirror to reflect light and
illuminate your face, or used beneath
kitchen wall units to give working areas
the practicality of good light. A
carefully position down-lighter or desk
lamp is ideal for close study such as
reading, writing or sewing.

Decorative lighting
Creates mood, producing the pools of
light which contrast with the
surrounding darkness to manufacture
atmosphere, and focus attention on
paintings or art objects. This is best
used in rooms where you wish to relax,
such as sitting-rooms and bedrooms, or
where a sense of drama is required. In a
dining-room, for instance, angled
down-lighters highlighting drapes or
table tops, give sharp illumination and
prominence to key room features.
Avoid using up-lighters and spots
where the plaster maybe uneven or in
poor condition, as the directional beam
will highlight these flaws.

SUPPLIERS

The Country Diary Collection Participating Licencees

LAMPS, LAMPSHADES, BASES

Alma Lighting Limited
Fishers Green Centre
Stevenage
Herts SG1 2PS

THIMBLES, COLLECTOR'S PLATES, FINE BONE CHINA GIFTWARE

Caverswall China Co Ltd
Berry Hill Road
Stoke-on-Trent
ST4 2PQ

David Shaw Silverware (NA) Ltd
4630 Dufferin Street
Unit 12a
Downsview
Ontario M3H 5S4
Canada

Fine English China Co
322 Sarassota Business Park
4233 Clark Road
Sarassota
Florida
USA

FLAT AND MOULDED MELAMINE FOR KITCHEN AND DINING-ROOM

Clover Leaf Ltd
Arkwright Road
Groundwell
Swindon
Wiltshire SN2 5BB

Clover Leaf Inc
RD5 McKee Road
PO Box 1489
Dover
Delaware 19903
USA

G Precious & Sons Ltd
1072 Hamilton Street
Vancouver BC
Canada

PARTY PAPERWARE

Deeko plc
Garman Road
London N17 0UG

BEDLINEN, TOWELS, KITCHEN TEXTILES, CURTAINS AND BLINDS, WALLPAPERS, DUVETS, PILLOWS, DECORATIVE BED CUSHIONS

Dorma
(CV Home Furnishings)
Newton Mill
Lees Street
Swinton
Manchester M27 2DD

GREETINGS CARDS, GIFT WRAP, BOOK-MARK TAGS

Elgin Court Designs
Units 1 & 3
Shepherd Road
Gloucester
GL2 6EL

FOOD

English Provender
Aldreth Farm
Haddenham
Isle of Ely
Cambridgeshire
CB6 3PG

English Provender Company Inc
6050 Boulevard East
Lobby Level, Suite F
West New York
NJ 07093
USA

Goods Trading Company
35 East Beaver Creek Road
Richmond Hill
Ontario
Canada L4B 1B3

CHOCOLATE EASTER EGGS, CONFECTIONERY

Jamesons Chocolates Plc
Willoughby Lane
Tottenham
London
N17 0RX

HERB PILLOWS, SPICE ROPES AND RIBBONS, TOILETRY TEXTILES

Kitty Little Ltd
Unit 5/6 Llewellyn Roberts Way
Market Drayton
Shropshire
TF9 1QS

Drummers West Limited
442 Nelo Street
PO Box 4697
Santa Clara
CA 95054
USA

Town Distributors Limited
5710 Royalmount Avenue
Montreal
H4P 1K5
Canada

CURTAIN AND UPHOLSTERY FABRICS

Moygashel Ltd
Moygashel Mills
Dungannon
County Tyrone
Northern Ireland
BT71 7QS

Dearne Mills
Darton
Barnsley
South Yorkshire
ST5 5PS

8517 Waters Point Court
Charlotte NC
USA

33 Hampton Drive
Kohimarama
Auckland
New Zealand

Northwold
PO Box 685
Gormley
Canada
LOH IGO

Overseas Marketers (Aust) Pty Ltd
65 Cambridge Street
Collingwood
Victoria
Australia

WILD FLOWER SEEDS

Norfolk Industries for the Blind
95 Oak Street
Norwich
NR3 3BP

FITTED KITCHEN UNITS, BEDROOM UNITS, WARDROBES, CHESTS, DRESSING-TABLES, BEDSIDE CABINETS AND SOLID WOOD HEADBOARDS

Solent Furniture Ltd
Pymore Mills
Bridport
Dorset
DT6 5PJ

TRAYS (FABRIC CASED IN PLASTIC)

Thetford Moulded Products Ltd
Mill Lane
Thetford
Norfolk
IP24 3DA

SOCIAL STATIONERY AND GIFTS, PHOTOGRAPH ALBUMS AND FRAMES, GIFT-WRAP PACKS AND TAGS, PENS, RING BINDERS, PORTFOLIOS, BLANK NOTEBOOKS

Waldorf Stationery
(Hestair-Hope Ltd)
PO Box 59
Royton Ring Mill
Royton
Oldham
Lancs
OL2 6AG

WALLCOVERINGS

Weston Hyde Products Ltd
(Vymura International Ltd)
PO Box 15
Cartwright Street
Hyde
Cheshire
SK14 4EJ

SLIPPERS

Pirelli Ltd
Derby Road
Burton-on-Trent
Staffs
DE13 0BH

Country Diary International Licencees

USA

Country Cross Stitch Inc
1937 Raymond Diehl Road
Tallahassee
Florida 32308
USA

Minnetonka
PO Box 1A
Minnesota 55343
USA

Noritake
75 Seaview Drive
Secaucus
NJ 07094
USA

NEW ZEALAND

Blair & Kent
Nelson House
Corner of Nelson & Wellesley Streets
PO Box 5492
Auckland
New Zealand

AUSTRALIA

Coloroll (Australia) Pty Ltd
1/8 Aquatic Drive
Frenchs Forest
NSW 2086
Australia

THAILAND

Srithai Superware Co Ltd
355 Sukwawat Road
S01 36 Bangapok
Rasburana
Bangkok
Thailand

SUPPLIERS

JAPAN

Isetan Company Ltd
14–1 Shinjuku 3-Chome
Shinjuku-ku
Tokyo
Japan

SOUTH AFRICA

Horrockses SA (Pty) Ltd
PO Box 306
Paarl
Cape 7620
South Africa

GERMANY

F W Heye Verlag GmbH
Ottobrunner Strasse 26-28
8025 Unterhaching
Postfach 1280
West Germany

CREDITS

SPRING

Page 14
Photography by Michael Crockett,
Elisabeth Whiting Associates

Page 15
The Greenway Hotel
Shurdington
Cheltenham
Glos GL51 5UG

Page 16
Photography Courtesy of Dulux,
ICI Paints

Dulux Australia Ltd
PO Box 60
Clayton
Victoria 3168
Australia

C-I-L Inc
PO Box 200
Station A
North York
Ontario M2N 6H2
Canada

Gliddon Co
925 Euclid Avenue
Cleveland
Ohio 0844116
USA

AECI
PO Box 1122
2000 Johannesburg
South Africa

ICI New Zealand Ltd
PO Box 31–048
Lower Hutt
Christchurch
New Zealand

Page 17
Solent Furniture Ltd

Page 18
Dorma

Page 19
Photograph by Tom Leighton,
Elisabeth Whiting Associates

Page 20 below
Photograph courtesy of Smallbone
Kitchens

Page 21
Photograph by Tom Leighton,
EWA

Page 22
Photograph courtesy of Smallbone
Bathrooms

Page 23
Country Diary *Meadow* by
Dorma/Vymura

Page 24
Photograph courtesy of BC
Sanitan

Page 26 above
Woodstock Furniture
Pakenham Street
London WC1X 0LB

Page 27
Crown Wallcoverings
Belgrave Mills
Darwin
Lancs

Page 28
Cabbage Rose fabric and Misty
Morning wallpaper from Anna
French, 343 Kings Road, London
SW3

Page 29
Wallpapers available from:
Vymura International
A Division of Weston Hyde
Products Ltd
PO Box 15
Hyde
Cheshire

Page 35
Bella Figura
154 Fulham Road
London SW10

Page 37 above
Manfred Schotten Antiques
The Crypt
109 High Street
Burford
Oxon OX8 4RH

Page 38 above
Photograph by Jerry Tubby, EWA

Page 38 below
Photograph courtesy of Dulux

Page 39
Country Diary *Wildflowers* by
Dorma/Vymura

Page 40 above
Maypole Collection by Designers
Guild
271/277 Kings Road
London SW3 5EN

Osborne & Little
Suite 1503N – 15th Floor
D & N Building
979 Third Avenue
New York
USA

Habert Associates Ltd
321 Davenport Road
Toronto
Ontario M5R 1K5

Rivtex
PO Box 153
Rose Bay
NSW
Australia

Mokum Textiles Ltd
11 Cheshire Street
Parnell
Auckland 1
New Zealand

Selwyn Neiman Pty Ltd
Nedbank Hall – 5th Floor
35 Siemart Road
Doornfontein
Johannesburg
South Africa

below
Photograph courtesy of Crown
Paints

Page 41
Country Diary *Honeysuckle Rose* by
Dorma/Vymura

Page 43 left
Vymura International
right
Dorma

Page 44
Photograph by Michael Dunne,
EWA

Page 45 below
Dulux
above
Vymura International

Page 46–47
Amdega Ltd
Faverdale
Darlington
County Durham DL3 0PW

Amdega Inc
Suite No 642
Boston Design Centre
Boston
Massachusetts 02210
USA

Page 48
The English Garden Collection
Machin Designs Ltd
Ransome's Dock
Parkgate Road
London SW11 4NP

Page 49 above
Conservatory by Marston & Langinger
George Edwards Road
Fakenham
Norfolk NR21 8NL

SUMMER

Page 52
Classique from Masonite CP Ltd
West Wing
Jason House
Kerry Hill
Horsforth
Leeds LS18 4JR

Masonite Corporation
1 South Wacker Drive
Chicago
IL 60606
USA

Page 54 both
Country Diary *Wildflowers* by Dorma/Vymura

Page 55
Photograph courtesy of Smallbone Kitchens

Page 56
Photograph courtesy of Dulux

Page 60
Country Diary *Springtime* by Vymura/Moygashel

Page 61
Country Diary *Honeysuckle Rose* by Dorma/Vymura

Page 62
Vintage suite and cast-iron bath from Vernon Tutbury Ltd
Fordham House
Dudley Road
Wolverhampton
WV2 4DS

Page 63
Photograph courtesy of BC Sanitan

Page 64
Sofabed from Sofasogood
Unit 7 Merton Industrial Estate
Morden Road
London SW19

Page 65 above
Photograph by Michael Dunne, EWA
below
Maypole Collection from Designers Guild

Page 68–69
Photograph by Fritz Von Der Schulenberg, designed by Lady Maureen Dudley

Page 70
Photograph courtesy of Smallbone Kitchens

Page 71 above
Photograph by Michael Nicholson, EWA

Page 72 above
Photography by Keith Lovegrove and Andrew Hasson for Damask, Unit 10, Sulivan Enterprise Centre, Sulivan Road, London SW6 3BS
below
Country Diary *Midsummer* by Dorma/Vymura

Page 73
Country Diary *Summer Scent* by Dorma/Vymura

Page 74
Country Diary *Honeysuckle Rose* by Dorma/Vymura

Page 75
Vymura International

Page 76
Country Diary *Wild Pear* by Vymura

Page 77
Dorma

Page 78
Camera Press, London

Page 79 both
Vymura International

Page 80 above
Country Diary *Wildflowers* by Vymura/Moygashel

Page 81 above
Country Diary *Flora* by Vymura/Moygashel

Page 81 below
Ornamenta Ltd
PO Box 784
London SW7 2TG

Clarence House
211 East 58th Street
NY 10022
New York
USA

Fowler Imports Pty Ltd
46 Queen Street
Woollahra
Sydney
NSW 2025
Australia

AUTUMN

Page 88 above
Needwood pine wash-stand and Chiltern vanity basin from Vernon Tutbury
below
Country Diary *Poppies* by Vymura/Moygashel

Page 90 above
Dorma

Page 91
Country Diary *Poppies* by Vymura/Moygashel

Page 94
Woodstock Furniture Ltd

Page 95 above
Photograph by Jerry Tubby, EWA
below
Classique by Hardboard Servicing

Page 97 below
Damask

Page 98
Country Diary *Poppies* by Dorma/Vymura

Page 99
Richmond cast-iron bath from Vernon Tutbury

Page 100
Needwood wash-stand and Vintage basin from Vernon Tutbury

Page 101
Photograph by Carol Sellers, EWA

Page 102 above
Rose designed by William Morris 1883 from Sanderson

Arthur Sanderson & Sons
Suite 403
979 Building
3rd Avenue
New York 10022
USA

Arthur Sanderson & Sons
99 Tuscan Gate
Downsview
Ontario
M3J 2T5
Canada

below
Woodstock Furniture Ltd

Page 103
Sue Stowell Wallpapers & Fabrics
765 Henley Road
Slough Trading Estate
Slough
Berks SL1 4JW

Page 104
Country Garden Collection by Kenneth Turner Designs for Dovedale Fabrics Ltd
Caerphilly Road
Ystrad Mynach
Hengoed
Mid Glamorgan CF8 7EP

Kirk Brumel Associates
826 Broadway
New York NY 10003
USA

Colefax and Fowler
46 Queen Street
Woollahra
Sydney NSW 2025
Australia

Page 105
Ornamenta

Page 106 above
English Country Cottages Ltd
Claypit Lane
Fakenham
Norfolk NR21 8AS
below
Oakleaf Reproductions Ltd
Wilsden
Bradford BD15 0JP

John Keller Associates
PO Box 13151
Webster Groves
Missouri 63119
USA

Page 107
Colefax & Fowler
39 Brook Street
London W1

Cowtan & Tout
D&D Building
979 3rd Avenue
NY 10022
USA

Colefax & Fowler
46 Queen Street
Woollahra
Sydney
NSW 2025
Australia

Page 108
Oakleaf Reproductions

Page 109 left
Colefax & Fowler

Page 110 above
Crown Paints
below
Country Garden Collection by Kenneth Turner for Dovedale Fabrics

Page 112
Country Diary *Poppies* by Dorma/Vymura

Page 114
And So To Bed
638–640 Kings Road
London SW6 2DU

Page 115 above
Country Diary *Wildflowers* by
Dorma/Vymura
below
Country Diary *Autumntide* by
Dorma/Vymura
Photograph by David Garcia,
styled by Francesca Mills. First
seen in *Country Living* magazine

Page 118 above
Carolyn Warrender Stencils
91–93 Lower Sloane Street
London SW1W 8DA
below
Photograph courtesy of Ronseal
15 Churchfield Court
Churchfield
Barnsley S70 2LJ

Page 119 below
Damask

WINTER

Page 125 above
Holly Lodge Hotel
Heacham
King's Lynn
Norfolk PE31 7HY
below left
Photograph by Spike Powell, EWA

Page 126
Ercol Furniture Ltd
High Wycombe
Bucks HP13 7AE

Page 127 above
Photograph by Clive Helm, EWA
below
Acres Farm Fenders
Acres Farm
Bradfield
Reading
Berks RG7 6HJ

Page 128–9
Photograph by Ron Sutherland,
EWA

Page 130
Photograph courtesy of Smallbone
Kitchens

Page 131
John Lewis of Hungerford
Unit 2
Limborough Road
Wantage
Oxon OX12 9AJ

Page 135
John Lewis of Hungerford

Page 136
Nauticalia Ltd
Ferry Lane
Shepperton-on-Thames
Middlesex TW17 9LQ

Page 140
Country Diary *Autumntide* by
Dorma/Vymura
Photograph by David Garcia,
styled by Francesca Mills. First
seen in *Country Living* magazine

Page 141
Combe House Hotel
Gittisham
Honiton
Devon

Page 142
Oakleaf Reproductions

Page 144
Ornamenta

Page 145 below
Crown Wallcoverings

Page 146
Damask

Page 147
Vymura

Page 148
Photograph by Michael Dunne,
EWA

Page 149
Dorma

Page 150
Damask

Page 151 above
Photograph by Michael Dunne,
EWA
below
And So to Bed

Page 152
Edward Russell Decorative
Accessories Ltd
18–20 Scrutton Street
London EC2A 4RJ

Edward Russell Decorative
Accessories Ltd
Gallery 726
225 Fifth Avenue
New York 10010
USA

Photographs on pages 15, 20, 25,
26, 42, 53, 57, 66, 93, 111, 124, 132,
137, 139 by Simon McBride

All additional photographs by
Sydney Sykes and
David McFadyan

Line drawings by Sydney Sykes

ACKNOWLEDGEMENTS

The *Country Diary Book of Decorating* would not have been possible without the assistance, enthusiasm and help of many friends and colleagues. Their names are too numerous to mention in full and I sincerely apologize for any omissions.

I would like to offer my special thanks to photographers David McFadyen and Simon McBride; designer Debra Dooly for her work on the blitz boards; Doreen Varley for her time and patience with the typing of the text; Michelle Lovric for her enthusiasm and advice; colleagues at C V Home Furnishings; Annette Sykes for her drawings of cushions; Ron Pickless for design layout and Alyson Gregory for editing the text.

In addition I must thank the many friends who have inspired me with their interest and enthusiasm, particularly while photographing their homes.

I thank especially Judith and Terry Lees; Judith and David Brandon; Pat and John Sergeant; Olive and Frank Wass; Stanley Bates, David Cordon and Michael Elles; Michael Bunn; Peter and Kathryn Nicholls; the Seckford Hall Hotel, The Bealings, Woodridge, Suffolk. And finally Woolpit Interiors, The Street, Woolpit, Bury St Edmunds, Suffolk IP 30 9SA. Tel: (0359) 40895.